Someone
Right for You

Edward A. Dreyfus, Ph.D

Human Services Institute
Bradenton, Florida

TAB BOOKS
Blue Ridge Summit, PA

Human Services Institute publishes books on human problems, especially those affecting families and relationships: addiction, stress, alienation, violence, parenting, gender, and health. Experts in psychology, medicine, and the social sciences have gained invaluable new knowledge about prevention and treatment, but there is a need to make this information available to the public. Human Services Institute books help bridge the information gap between experts and people with problems.

FIRST EDITION
FIRST PRINTING

Published by HSI and TAB Books.
TAB Books is a division of McGraw-Hill, Inc.

Library of Congress Cataloging-in-Publication Data

Dreyfus, Edward A., 1937-
    Someone Right for You / by
Edward A. Dreyfus
        p. cm.
    Includes index.
    ISBN 0-8306-3969-1   ISBN 0-8306-3087-2 (pbk.)
    1. Love.   2. Interpersonal relations.   3. Intimacy (Psychology)
I. Title.
HQ801.D76   1992
306.7—dc20   91-35596
                                                                    CIP

TAB Books offers software for sale. For information and a catalog, please contact TAB Software Department, Blue Ridge Summit, PA 17294-0850.

Questions regarding the content of this book should be addressed to:

Human Services Institute, Inc.
P.O. Box 14610
Bradenton, FL 34280

Acquisitions Editor: Kimberly Tabor
Development Editor: Lee Marvin Joiner, Ph.D.   HSI

Contents

Acknowledgments

It is with sincere appreciation that I acknowledge the invaluable contribution of Joel Engel who helped transform my ideas from academic prose into a readable style. I am grateful to my editor, Dr. Lee Marvin Joiner, without whose support, encouragement, and enthusiasm this book would never have been published. And lastly, I wish to thank all of my patients who permitted me to share in their journey of self-discovery and from whom I have learned so much about the human struggle for intimacy.

You have probably tried many different approaches to meeting the person of your dreams and, like so many diets, they just don't work for you. And neither will this approach work for you: *You must work for it.* It will only be effective if you make a commitment to see it through. You may be sincere in your desire to find romance, but are you committed to finding romance? What's the difference? Sincerity refers to your intent, to your desire, to what is in your heart. Commitment is what you do. You may sincerely want to lose weight, but you still reach for the chocolate; you may be sincere, but you are not committed. You want the immediate satisfaction of the chocolate—you want it now! You are committed to getting the chocolate regardless of the consequences, but you are not committed to losing weight. Likewise, you may be sincere in your desire to find a mate, but are you committed— committed enough to read this book through with an open mind; committed enough to do the suggested excersises? Committed enough to change?

It is time for a radical change in your approach to finding romance. If your approach worked for you, you would not have bought this book. Too often we settle for that which is simply comfortable despite the fact that it does not make us happy. My approach is different. And like all different ideas, it may feel uncomfortable. You must try it on, just as you would a new hair style or cuisine, and it might take a while to get adjusted. Don't settle for comfort when you want change. Comfort breeds complacency; action breeds change.

If you are open to change and are willing to take a few risks, you should find the approach outlined in these pages fun, exciting, and rewarding. You will learn a great deal about yourself. Have fun and be creative. You are about to begin in a journey of discovery.

E. A. D.

Part I

Making Romance Happen

Refugees from Romance

Relationships are in trouble. Divorce is on the increase, fewer people are marrying, and complaints about current relationships are rampant. Men and women decry the scarcity of available partners. People seem to repeat mistakes made in prior relationships even after vowing "I'll never make that mistake again!" We don't seem to learn from our mistakes when it comes to relationships; rather we seem to repeat them.

We hear the term codependence, which originally came from those mental health professionals who deal with such addictions as alcoholism, drugs, and eating disorders. The concept referred to the persons whose lives were affected as a result of being involved with someone who was addicted (dependent) to some substance. The term has been broadened to include the process by which partners, relatives, and friends may be participating in the addiction of another person. The most obvious example of this is when a spouse, after complaining about his or her mate's drinking problem, goes out and buys a six-pack while doing the grocery shopping. In relationships, the term is applied to those persons who contribute to the difficulty in a relationship by subtly encouraging the very behaviors that are the basis for the problems. Codependence also refers to the repeated choosing of similar partners who fulfill unconscious needs, despite the destructiveness of the relationship. Thus abused women often choose abusive men. Hen-pecked men choose women who will dominate them, and then complain about the domination without examining their own participation.

Many of the patterns for choosing a mate were laid down during childhood. We tend to emulate parts of the relationships we observed during childhood, most predominantly those of our parents. Often we will try to avoid certain aspects of those relationships while inadvertently imitating others. For example, we can vow we will not do the things that one parent does while not being aware of the effect the other parent is having on us. We subsequently may choose the less dominant parent as a mate in the future ending up in a similar place as our parents. Another uncanny aspect of this process is the fact that we can choose a mate that is like our same-sexed parent as well as the opposite-sexed parent. That is, men can marry women like their fathers, as well as their mothers; and women can marry men like their fathers as well as their mothers.

People who come from dysfunctional families often involve themselves in codependent relationships. Their dysfunctional family, in effect, programs them to choose and behave in relationships in ways that tend to support their original concept of relationships.

Earnie Larson, an expert in the field of codependence, has defined codependency as "those self-defeating, learned behaviors or character defects that result in a diminished capacity to initiate, or to participate, in loving relationships." It also has been said that he has defined codependence as "any romantic relationship with a neurotic."

Paul Bohannan, a cultural anthropologist at the University of Southern California, who has spent the last four decades studying divorce, states, "When you select your own spouse, you unconsciously choose someone who will shore up your own weak points or fulfill your special needs or neurosis. If you choose someone on that basis, it can blind you to the real qualities of the other person. You project qualities onto your partner that aren't really there. Then, once you realize the person you fell in love with isn't who you thought he was, he's a skunk."

After reading much of this it all sounds pretty dismal. How are we going to get out of this mess? Are all relationships doomed even before they start? Is it all hopeless? Are we doomed to repeat old patterns until we resolve all of the underlying issues affecting our choices? I do not think so.

There are many self-help books on the market dealing with relationships. One would think that these experts would have the answer to the dilemma of wanting relationships, on the one hand, and finding them painful on the other.

Many authors deal with how to live with a neurotic. These books tell us how we can develop ourselves so that we will feel better about ourselves and enhance our self-esteem. The feminist authors argue against romantic love. They say that women will adjust, modify, and twist themselves to fit into the concept of romantic love, much like they modify parts of their body in order to fit a male concept of beauty. The solution they suggest is to get rid of the notion of romantic love as oppressive. Women seem willing to subordinate parts of themselves in order to maintain a relationship with a neurotic or inappropriate mate; they adjust to a bad situation and hence perpetuate the situation. They believe that they are doomed to repeat relationships and that romantic love is the problem.

Psychoanalytic approaches (insight oriented) say "know yourself better and you will make better choices." Cognitive theory, on the other hand, suggests that you "make better choices and you will change patterns and feelings." People need to learn new patterns of thinking and behaving. Insight, while necessary, is not enough. Action is also necessary.

The emphasis of this book is on action. The belief is that while it is fruitful and necessary to understand your beliefs, and that getting in touch with your feelings is helpful and even necessary, these approaches alone will not effect change in your choices.

If you are looking to dramatically affect your life in ways that really matter, action is necessary. Listening to the feelings of the inner child who is afraid of making decisions, afraid of abandonment and rejection, and is a victim of abuse, is not in and of itself bad, if the listening is for the purpose of gaining greater self-awareness. Nevertheless, if you accept his or her feelings as valid for your present life, you will not act. And if you wait until the inner child is healed you will not have the life you want or deserve today. An alternative approach is to act and change your beliefs on the basis of the action you took. Feelings and beliefs will change when action is taken and the expected catastrophic consequences do not occur.

When it comes to relationships, we tend to rely on antiquated information obtained in childhood. In effect, the child is making the decisions for the adult. The child has certain perceptions of relationships based on the interpretations that the child makes. Children, however, do not have the ability to grasp the subtleties of adult interactions. Their development is not sufficient to understand adult sexuality, for example. Yet we base our relationships on the understandings of the child.

Most of our intimate relationships are based on childhood experiences, feelings, and beliefs. In order to change we must use adult tools. We must develop a plan of action similar to the action plan that we would use for any other adult undertaking, such as looking for a job, planning a career, buying a house or car, hiring an employee, or building a business or house.

In these activities, we utilize different skills than when we are involved in seeking an appropriate mate. The approach used in these areas were developed by adults in an attempt to deal with adult reality. Hopefully, we do not plan a career, a business, or buy a house based on the beliefs and fantasies of the child. We want to reconceptualize romantic love to show that cognition plays a role without eliminating romance, love, and intimacy.

Our current concept of romance and mate selection is heavily influenced by our childhood, our parents, television, movies, and books. Most of the information obtained in childhood is based on the child's or adolescent's understanding of adult relationships. Information gleaned from movies, television, and books is based on a screen-writer's or director's conception of reality and of what will sell. The author, writer, or director is the one influenced by his or her own life experiences. Most of the romantic love stories reflect the fantasies of their authors. Thus we find ourselves in the untenable position of trying to make our reality live up to these childhood conceptions and adult fantasies. In order to have a fulfilling and rewarding relationship there must be concordance between our reality and the actions we take. We must act in ways that move toward the results we wish to obtain. Relationships must fit the reality in which we live. There is no one single concept of relationship suitable to all people as television, romantic novels, and movies would have us believe.

This book will help you develop a strategy for making better choices. It will guide you through the steps necessary for you to discover your own needs, wishes, and expectations. It will help you to decide whether your expectations are realistic. Then it will help you develop a personalized action plan for seeking the persons—yes, persons, there is more than one available to you— appropriate for you. The first step, however, is to develop a plan.

If I am building a dream house, I will first create a blueprint. The house must be appropriate for the lot upon which it is to be built. Not every design would be appropriate for each lot. Also, the design must suit my particular lifestyle. I have to think about the way I live my life, what size and how many rooms I may need, how they should be laid out, and so on. And then I have to decide on style, number of stories, lighting, windows, doors, and the rest. Only after I have spent considerable time in developing the plans will I begin the construction. I must be willing to modify the plan as I collect more information. But I must not deviate from the plan in an impulsive way just because I found some attractive set of doors or windows, for it might destroy the functional integrity of the house. If you follow your plan, you will love your dream house and will have learned a great deal about yourself in the process.

A similar approach will be taken throughout this book for finding a mate. Once you develop your plan thoughtfully, you must stick to it. Consult the plan when you are in doubt and choose accordingly. The results will pay off and you will *love* your dream mate.

The messages of this book are:

- You can break the codependency cycle.
- You can learn to choose wisely and well.
- You do not have to eliminate romance from your life.
- There are many more possibilities than you think.
- Reason and romance are not mutually exclusive.
- Mate selection can be exciting and fun as well as an opportunity for self-discovery.

Radical Rethinking

Most of us seem to get along reasonably well despite the complexities of modern life. For the problems of finding a job, a house, a car, a brass fitting for the bathroom sink, we use commonsense methods that have worked in the past, either for ourselves or someone we know. Yet when the pursuit involves romance and mating, all reason and experience are abandoned. Finding an acceptable mate, for most people, is as scientific as turning straw into gold.

SOMEONE SPECIAL

People assume I know a horde of eligible singles, perhaps because I am a clinical psychologist. At cocktail parties and in other social situations, they often ask me to fix them up with "someone special." My response usually takes them by surprise.

Instead of materializing a black book containing the names of five hundred or so "someone specials," I ask two short but important questions: "What are you looking for in a mate?" and "How are you now going about finding that particular person?"

The first question is typically met with a kind of blank stare, followed by a stammering, vague response: "Well, you know," say the women, "someone who's nice, and makes a lot of money." And the men say, "Well, you know, someone who's good looking and sexy."

To the second question, the answer from both sexes is an even blanker stare, followed by, "Well, you know, the usual places."

These answers indicate two things: that most singles have given little or no thought to the process of mating, and that a tremendous discrepancy exists between what people say and what they do about mating. While, on the one hand, they claim to be serious about finding a steady romantic partner, they really do not pursue that goal as energetically as they would almost anything else important in their lives—jobs and housing and cars, for example.

There is an irony here. While we consider it proper to plan thirty years—through high school, college, post-graduate studies, and apprenticeships—for a career, we generally leave mate selection to chance. We applaud achievements that rely on hard work and dedication, but our most cherished notion about romance remains love-at-first-sight. Either it happens, we say, or it doesn't.

ARE YOU WAITING FOR LOVE?

Movies, music and literature all celebrate the magic that occurs when two strangers, transformed by a thunderbolt, suddenly and mystically unite. Think of the thousands of Technicolor images and stereophonic melodies, pounded relentlessly into our brains and memories over the years, whose heroes and heroines met apparently by the hands of fate. Those who set out consciously to meet a mate were most often portrayed as schemers or manipulators, and they usually failed in their quests. It's no wonder we have become hypnotized into believing that if we wait long enough, "Our Day Will Come . . ."

All of us are victims of such manufactured myths. Our own experiences of love and romance and relationships are judged against these powerful messages—whether they be from Hans Christian Andersen, Cole Porter, or Cecil B. DeMille—and many of us wait our entire lives to be swept off our feet by that cosmic force. We trust that our heaven-sent lover is just around the next corner, wearing a sign that says, "I'm your one true love."

Some people wait in the secluded confines of their bedrooms and living rooms. Hidden from the rest of the world, they pray for a lover to materialize out of thin air. And each night when their true love fails to show, they are mystified—like the devoutly religious woman whose family had fallen on hard times financially. Seeing the lottery as one way to solve their problems, she went to church, where she prayed fervently: "Oh God, I beg you, please help us to win the lottery."

She did the same the following week, increasing the tone of desperation in her voice. "Oh Lord," she said, "I beg you, I beseech you, I humble myself before you— please help us to win the lottery."

Still penniless, she entered the church week after week, at times crying in the hopes of attracting God's attention. One day, after a particularly fervent prayer for help, came a blinding flash of light and crashing thunder. "Barbara," boomed the voice from above, "meet me halfway—buy a ticket."

From a purely logical viewpoint, such pray-and-do-nothing behavior seems absurd at best, yet millions of people from of all backgrounds, all intelligence levels, and all professions are guilty of it. Many end up spending their lives alone, because in the real world people rarely happen upon their true love, or they settle for anyone who comes along. One man I know, the vice president of marketing for one of the largest industrial corporations in the United States, is responsible for cooking up the most imaginative strategies intended to get products to millions of consumers. As smart as he is, he returns unsuccessfully time and again to the same handful of singles bars to meet the woman of his dreams. I have little doubt that if he were to implement such a spectacularly narrow-minded plan at his job, he would be fired immediately; inasmuch as his goal is romance, his actions—or inactions—are considered entirely acceptable.

Leaving something as important as mating to sheer chance is inconsistent with the desire to couple. That type of passiveness actually runs contrary to our natural tendencies to satisfy our needs. For instance, if you wanted a new pair of shoes, would you sit at home and wait for them to be delivered? If you were in the market for a couch, would you stand on a street corner, hoping a moving van might accidentally drop one you like? Of course you wouldn't, because you're in the habit of going after what you want; you don't sit idly awaiting its arrival. Only when the desire is for romance do we abandon logic in favor of the supernatural. We have been taught to believe that love and mating are ordained.

Well, not everything we ever learned is necessarily healthy, correct, or productive. Remember that at one time slavery was considered to be just another fact of life, and that women were inherently inferior. While mating certainly can't compare with these examples in moral or historical importance, the lessons we all learned about helplessness in mating must be questioned and unlearned.

Consider the story of a man whose home was being destroyed by raging flood waters. He climbed out of his window and up onto the roof, where he sat and waited. A small motorboat pulled alongside. "Climb in and I'll take you to high ground," said the would-be rescuer. "No thanks," said the man, "I'm waiting for God to save me." A while later, with the flood waters still rising, another boat approached. Once again, the man refused the offer to take him to safety by declaring, "I'm waiting for God to save me." Half an hour later, with the waters now danger-ously close to the roof, a helicopter hovered over the man's house. "We'll drop you a line," boomed the pilot's voice. "Grab on and we'll lift you out of there." "No thanks," said the man. "I'm waiting for God to save me." Well, the flood waters rose higher than the roof, swept the man away, and he drowned. Arriving in heaven, he told God that he couldn't understand why he hadn't been saved. "What are you talking about?" said God. "I sent you two boats and a helicopter."

While good things may indeed come to those who wait, opportunities are meant to be grabbed; if you know where and how to look for them, the world is full of oppor-tunities.

A RECIPE FOR ROMANCE

Both love-at-first-sight and marriages-made-in-heaven are no more metaphysical than gravity. Think of the people you know who claim they searched in vain for years trying to find a suitable mate, and then one day, "as if by magic," met their future bride or groom. If you study those situations through a narrow lens, they look like lucky people who finally hit the jackpot. Only through a wider angle can the real dynamics be observed. The force that brought these people together was not some mysterious alchemy that touches some people and not others. Rather it was the reaction created by a fitting combination of interests, attitudes, and outlooks.

Try visualizing the process as a sort of recipe for romance. Each of us is the sum of certain ingredients —thoughts, feelings, and experiences—which cause us subliminally to give out signals, messages, and vibrations. If, under the proper circumstances, one person's ingredients are mixed together with another whose ingredients are compatible, the result seems magically delicious. The participants who have fallen in love will be unaware of what caused them to feel as they do, but the process took place all the same.

Many reject this concept at first. They believe that true love is a spontaneous, natural and beautiful stream that flows between two people lucky enough to have been touched. Of course it is, and I'm not trying to reduce it to an equation mapped out by a super computer. My contention is simply this: The number of people out there in the world with whom any of us has a reasonable chance of nurturing a serious romantic relationship is not infinitely large, and we ought to make better use of our time to find those who might fit well with us by following a clear and consistent plan.

Gary Knew Exactly What He Wanted . . . and Got It

Gary, a college friend, had grown up in poverty. While extremely motivated to succeed on his own, he also wanted to be certain that his wife came from a wealthy family, just in case. "It's as easy to fall in love with a rich girl as a poor one," he told me time and again. His strategy, which he followed diligently, was to investigate the father of any girl he began to get interested in. He would contact Dun and Bradstreet, the company which provides financial ratings of businesses and individuals, continuing to date the girl only if her father was rated, and maintained a plus rating. "If I don't check him out," he said, "I might fall in love and then find out her father is a street cleaner." As it turned out, Gary ended up meeting, falling deeply in love with, and marrying the daughter of one of New York's most influential investment bankers. Having studied finance in school, he stepped right into a lucrative job at the firm.

Gary succeeded because he surrounded himself with the type of women who fit his target group, and then when romance struck, he was able to follow his heart; he did not marry for money, he married for love a woman who had money. Likewise, college students who decide to join a fraternity rush several that fit their criteria, so it matters little which one accepts them.

IF YOU KNOW THE GAME, YOU CAN WIN

A plan does not preclude romance—the two are not mutually exclusive—it merely allows more opportunities. The planning refers simply to locating a possible mate(s), not to the courtship itself. What you do with your prospect(s) after that—whether it's fine wine, candles and Beethoven, or beer, pretzels, and Black Sabbath—is up to you.

All I'm trying to do is reduce the influence of luck in this, the mating game, and put more control over what happens to you into your own hands. As in any endeavor, by increasing our odds we improve our chances of winning. Abandoning the process to luck or chance relinquishes control over what may be your life's most important decision. Luck is something that happens to people who have worked hard to create opportunities.

What you will find in this book is not magic. Nor is it a collection of secrets that have been stored in some cave of the ancients. I offer proven cause-and-effect solutions to the problems of finding a suitable mate in a world that, otherwise, can be terribly inscrutable. I know my plan works because I've seen it work, time and again, with the patients in my practice. It was because of them, listening to hundreds of them over the years complain about their inability to find a mate, that I devised the plan.

Contained in this book is guidance for those serious about a finding a compatible mate. If followed diligently, the approach will work; you will meet people with whom you may want to become romantic. In the process, it may also reveal areas of self-knowledge that have been lurking shyly behind a facade of ignorance. And if that happens, well, so much the better. The more you know about yourself, the easier it is to get what you want.

Remember that marriage is a legal partnership. Your mate will become not only your lover, but your roommate, your business partner and possibly the parent of your children. Choosing a mate demands strategy, resolution, determination and patience, not the romantic notions portrayed in the movies. Some of you may need to do some radical rethinking, but my feeling is you wouldn't be reading these words right now if your old line of thought had been successful—and you weren't willing to try something new.

Using a proven step-by-step method, this book will instruct you how to meet many people with whom you have a reasonable and realistic chance of achieving romance—if that is indeed what you truly want. If it's not, this book will allow you to explore your true intentions. And if a series of casual playmates is what you want, then this book will show you how to go about finding your cream of the crop.

What About Falling in Love?

By necessity, our great-grandparents were more realistic, more pragmatic, about the mating process than we've become. To them, marriages were purely functional. Men and women were brought together, often blindly through a third party, as a business arrangement, for purposes of procreation, not recreation; romance was something that may or may not have come later. Marriages usually were for the sole purpose of raising a family, the members of which would produce economic benefits for the group, in addition to caring for the elderly. The arrangement was life insurance, disability insurance, and old age insurance in one neat, extended package.

As the post-Industrial Revolution society moved families away from the farm and into the cities, and technology began to replace manual labor, more leisure time became available to the average person. Into the vacuum created by that leisure flowed, among other things, romantic expectations, previously squelched by the hard realities of daily life. Now, it was no longer necessary to have a purely functional relationship. People wanted more because society itself extended that invitation: two cars in every garage, a chicken in every pot, and a heart kept warm by the hearth. Relationships became an end in themselves.

The criteria for relationships became such factors as sexual attraction, common interests and needs, intellectual and emotional compatibility, and a host of intangibles sometimes referred to collectively as "chemistry." So far, so good. Boys and girls met, married and had children. While they may have later divorced, the separation most likely occurred because the fires no longer burned between them. Although painful, at least the freedom to divorce was an improvement over the rigid and unbreakable bond between our ancestors, who stayed married, despite what could be a lifetime of unrelenting misery.

IN SEARCH OF A PERFECT PARTNER

Single people today who have trouble meeting and mating contend that it was easier in past eras to find a suitable partner. Well, they're probably right. And for plain reasons. We were then a less complex, less mobile society. With such added complexities as changing male and female roles, increased freedom of physical movement, and population decentralization in the urban areas, it is more difficult now to meet others with whom we have at least something in common. Our expectations about what constitutes a "good" relationship have undergone the most profound change. "She's a good woman" meant that she was a good housekeeper, cook, and mother; while "He's a good man" meant that he provided food and shelter for his family, didn't beat his wife, and didn't run around with other women.

Today, however, the women's rights movement, a vast and powerful economy, everpresent technology, and near-universal education have created an environment in which people believe that perfection is a divine right. The quest for the perfect relationship, the modern-day equivalent of the Holy Grail, causes people to look continually, believing that perfection will be found around the next corner. Ironically, we have come to believe that it is bad or unhealthy, or even impossible, to make romance happen—that is, to devise strategies more logical than hanging out in a place where a lot of singles congregate.

As the 1960s and 1970s focussed our attention on building technological marvels that relied only on a person's mental acuity, not brawn, the traditional lines of demarcation between men's work and women's work grew murkier. At the same time, the country's economy, plundered by the Vietnam War (which itself called into question most previously accepted morals and values), forced many families to seek second incomes just to survive at the level to which they'd grown accustomed. We had become a nation of consumers, and we wanted more, more, more. Coming directly from the days of the Civil Rights movement and Vietnam War protests, a snowballing momentum had been created to correct other social inequities wherever they could be found.

One of those inequities was the unequal treatment of women now working in a "man's world," and from the intention to correct that wrong came the new belief, affecting both sexes, that "You Can Have It All": a successful career, enough money to indulge every consumerism whim, and the perfect lover. For the generation born in the years immediately following World War II, "having it all" has become merely the standard expectation. Television's most popular program is *The Cosby Show*, in which a doctor and a lawyer are portrayed as always having quality time for each other and their five kids, while their beautiful home is always immaculately clean.

What those changes spell is confusion, if not chaos, for many. Men and women have both undergone major attitudinal shifts in the last generation. Competing for the same jobs and maintaining a higher consciousness about roles, males and females are uncertain how they should treat each other, professionally, socially and romantically. Their questioning of new role boundaries sometimes causes awkwardness, or even social paralysis. Finding a suitable mate has become an unbelievably complex task.

THE POWER OF SHARED EXPERIENCES

But the situation isn't irrevocably desperate. An examination of how males and females used to meet offers us some applicable insights that form the basis of a workable strategy for finding a mate. Adapting a few of the old techniques—that, whether it seems like it or not, were indeed techniques—can benefit our own search. And in the process, it can also justify to the skeptics why implementing a strategy for finding a mate is not antiromantic.

Shyness and social clumsiness aside (these will be dealt with at length later in the book), the time in most people's lives when they most easily met potential dates, and mates, was while they were in school. Why? The legwork, so to speak, had already been done for us. We attended the same school, comprised (more or less) the same age group, had the same (more or less) broad range of interests; at the very least, a conversation starter could be how hard Mrs. Krupnitz's history class was, or what a drag our parents were. We had common friends, and, sometimes more importantly, common enemies. In short, the pre-selection process had already been completed for us. Living in the same geographical location just about guaranteed that we'd be of similar economic and social backgrounds. School gave us all something in common, something we could draw on to break the ice. In the years before society became almost completely mobile and women's demands for full societal participation shook up our traditional role identifications, those common interests would usually be enough to begin the wedding march.

From this brief snatch of information, we can draw conclusions about the elements comprising a potentially successful pairing: common of interests, common purposes, similar geographical location.

Let's investigate these further.

A common task draws people together easier than con-trived situations in which the sole stated purpose is to meet in the hopes of bonding. Think of the blind dates you've had with people whom you knew nothing about other than, "He's (she's) nice." I could bet, with reasonable certainty of winning, that the rendezvous was stiff and uncomfortable.

If I decide to meet just "someone," who has also decided to meet just "someone," and we arrange a place and a time for the meeting, the tension when we get together will likely be high; periods of silence may be broken only by the question, "So, how's the weather where you're from?" On the other hand, should we be brought together by a shared experience, even something as mundane as shopping for tomatoes, we are allowed to communicate, rather than forced to, because the context in which the meeting takes place invites communication.

The connection between shared experience and com-munication can be seen even more clearly using sports fans as examples. Fans from cities that have professional sports franchises often scream obscenities at each other during a game solely because each affiliates himself with a different team. However, these same fans will root in unison when a team representing a geographical area encompassing both their cities plays against another team. In the Olympics, fans from Boston and New York, who threaten to nuke each other each time the Yankees play the Red Sox, became bosom buddies as quickly as they became hoarse, rooting together for the U.S. ice hockey team against the Soviets. The moral is that if people can overcome their apparently intense differences, as they do in rooting for sports teams, then those who are in opposition to each other because of something as simple as their appearance can be drawn together through shared experiences. And, *voila*, the possibilities for developing relationships are vastly increased.

THE TROUBLE WITH SINGLES BARS

We have become a culture of instant gratification. Hence, the singles bar, where the mass murderer on the next stool blinks shyly and asks if you're a Pisces. Nowhere is the idea of the uncommon denominator more apparent than in the singles bar. Why? Because people persist in maintaining that love is either something that happens to you or doesn't. So by hanging out where dozens of other people also want desperately to meet Mr. or Ms. Right, the chances are increased, right?

Wrong. If love does indeed come in lightning bolts, then singles bars are lightning rods, taking the electricity from the sky and grounding it harmlessly. Whatever or whomever you may pick up at a singles bar, love is not very likely to be included. They're fine for the person who isn't looking to mate seriously. Those who are might just as well wait at home for the heaven-sent lover to descend on a moonbeam as frequent singles bars.

Now, I don't mean to give the impression that all bars are poor breeding grounds for romance, because there are ways bars can be incorporated into your overall strategy for finding a mate. More about that later. What I'm talking about here is the quintessential, stereotypical singles bar, in essence the fast food restaurant aimed at satisfying our craving for instant gratification. Ask yourself: of all the great lovers in history—Romeo and Juliet, Anthony and Cleopatra, Liz and Dick—how many met at singles bars?

People generally get angry with this contention. Sure, most agree that these bars are no place to begin a lasting relationship, yet they continue to attend them with the high expectations that tonight could be the night. At the same time, these people, who claim that a serious relationship is their goal, will segregate their professional and social lives, believing that all budding romances are formed only in places built solely for socialization. Art lovers though they may be, for example, the art museum is rarely a place they think to go for meeting others with whom they have something in common; it may not occur to them that while they are admiring Matisse, they may also be an object of desire.

Their tenacious resistance to change comes from a deep-seated belief that love is magically ordained. "But what about falling in love?" they ask when told that a clear, precise strategy is needed to successfully increase the odds of meeting someone with whom they might mate. "I don't think you can regulate that sort of thing."

The irony is that these people don't question the so-called high school sweetheart syndrome, theorizing that the two young lovers who met and married at an early age because of their intense passion were predestined for each other. The process that joined them was in fact much less subtle, and more systematic, than it seemed.

For art lovers, after all, what could be more romantic than meeting in an art museum, surrounded by priceless treasures? That would be fine, say the skeptics on their way to the singles bar, if it just "happens." Suppose I were to tell the art-loving man who did just "happen" to meet a woman at an art gallery that the "chance" meeting that brought them together was actually the skillfully engineered end product of a conceptualized strategy by the woman. He might laugh, or, more likely, he'd disbelieve it.

Yet this same man had, in the distant past, waited around after school in front of a certain gate because he knew that a girl he liked from afar would soon be walking past. He may also have risked traffic accidents and speeding tickets to "just happen" to fill up with gasoline at the same station as a woman he saw driving in the other direction. "Those situations," he'll defend, "are different." As long as the plan to find a mate isn't a consciously sustained act, this reasoning would seem to say, it's acceptable; otherwise it's conniving.

Even in our language is that belief implicit. The phrases "on the make," "designing woman" and "man hungry," among others, all connote the feeling that searching rationally for a mate is, somehow, shameful.

To that I ask: Is it really so romantic to grope blindly in a darkened bar at last-call to find someone who can keep you warm? Is it really so romantic to scream small talk over blasting music? Is it really so romantic to stand meekly on the sidelines at a singles dance when your sex outnumbers the opposite three to one?

To me, and probably to you, romance may be eyes meeting across a darkened room, a candlelight dinner, a walk on the beach at sunset, a fireplace on a brisk night while sharing a bottle of wine. Well, none of these is precluded by an organized strategy for mating, nor by using logic to attain emotional rewards.

I think you and I could agree easily that by the time someone falls in love "at first sight" with a new home, perhaps dozens of other houses have already been inspected and considered. House-hunting is a process that almost everyone has experienced. Well, the methodical steps comprising a successful search are not that dissimilar from those of a successful mate hunt.

Before buying a home, the potential buyer decides how much he or she can afford; the preferred geographical location; how many bedrooms and bathrooms are needed; whether a backyard and front yard are necessary, and so forth. Other considerations may include architectural styles and potential for adding on later. Then the buyer discusses these qualifications with a real estate agent, who sifts through hundreds of listings to find those which fit the stated criteria. And together they look at some houses.

After weeks, maybe months, of visiting and revising and updating the criteria list to reflect more realistic expectations, one day the buyer falls in love, "magically, at first sight," with a particular house. Even then, several more visits are made to prove and validate those initial feelings before finally making an offer and buying.

Such an approach to finding a house, even a car, sounds reasonable enough to most people. Yet when I contend that something similar is appropriate to finding a mate, people respond strangely.

MIND, NOT MAGIC

If the idea of forming a strategy to find a mate seems abhorrent to you, you're probably still stuck in the idea that love either happens or doesn't, depending on luck. But if, as Edison said, "genius is ten percent inspiration and ninety percent perspiration," then you've got to get sweaty—metaphorically speaking, of course—to make it happen.

All your life you have been on the receiving end of other people's marketing strategies aimed at getting you to buy their products. Using elaborate preference surveys and testing responses to various colors and packaging, these marketing "geniuses" experiment with variables until they achieve the desired result: you, and millions of others, shell out money. That's not magic, it's strategy.

You have even packaged yourself, dressing and behaving in ways that you thought would make you most attractive to potential mates. Sometimes it worked and sometimes it didn't, depending, probably, on luck. But what separates consistent results from the luck of the draw, as the marketing geniuses know, is strategy—and that you didn't have. You lacked the tools with which to present your goods to a particular audience anxious to buy them, not to the masses at large. You need the ability to target a specific group and market yourself to it.

Those tools and abilities, that knowledge, are what this book is all about.

Are You Serious?

The person you want and can expect to find obviously depends on who you are. How, for example, can a woman standing five feet tall and weighing three hundred pounds realistically expect to meet and marry Mr. Universe? Yet I constantly hear the sad lament of profoundly unrealistic women like her who dismiss their male counterparts with a plump- handed wave. Or how about a man who says he's searching for a Marie Curie when he himself doesn't read anything more stimulating than *TV Guide*? Unless Madame is the type who wants an empty-headed appendage to stand in awe of her intellectual accomplishments, he surely faces a difficult task.

The truth is, such people are not serious about having a real flesh and blood relationship. These people know, in their heart of hearts, that their desires are unobtainable and unrealistic. But the child in them holds out with crossed fingers and rabbits' feet for the wave of a magic wand that will unite their fantasies with their inadequacies. They are more infatuated with the dream of a relationship than with ever having one. Their unwillingness to examine the facts truthfully and abandon the Fred Astaire-Ginger Rogers fairy tale provides a never-ending stream of excuses for being alone. No matter what they say, what they do, or don't do, speaks louder than their words.

Honestly now, how serious are you about finding a mate? Although the above examples seem somewhat exaggerated, there may be elements of truth in those representations that apply to you. While you may think and feel that a mate is the only missing ingredient in what would otherwise be a happy life, your deeds and actions might suggest something else.

Being serious about finding a mate means being clear about what you want in that person and realistic about your ability to attain that goal. It also means objectively analyzing your romantic history, no matter how long or short, for bits of information that could help you align your intentions with your actions.

SEPARATE FANTASY FROM REALITY

We all like to fancy ourselves the epitome of everything wonderful and great, according to our system of values. But for everyone I've ever known, the truth is distant from the fantasy. That goes equally for me. I often picture myself in the stereotypical professor role, reading Shakespeare in front of a roaring fireplace, smoking my pipe and sipping Cognac, my dog at my feet. When I'm really honest with myself, I admit that I'd much rather plop down in front of the boob tube, swilling beer and watching reruns of *Cagney and Lacey* (at least the part about the dog is true). Given the opportunity to live that professorial life, I'd be screamingly bored.

A patient told me that the type of woman he really wanted would be "homespun." Gil came to that conclusion after spending a week as the guest of a farm family.

Watching the traditional family unit operate, the wife up early cooking, the husband and children working the crops, aroused all sorts of paternal and domestic feelings in him. So when he returned to his job in the city, he concocted a comparably ideal scenario for himself.

I listened quietly as he described the idyllic life the four or five or six or seven of them would have in the country, "where it's so much simpler." Then I advised him to be realistic. He looked at me as though I'd drowned his cat. We both knew that Gil could no more have lived out his fantasy than he could fly by flapping his arms. Born in Detroit, raised in New York City, and working in Chicago, his idea of the pastoral life was a corned beef sandwich at a delicatessen in the suburbs. After being on a farm for less than a month, he'd probably have phoned his friends in the big city just to hear the impatient honks of taxicabs in the background. His desire for a homespun girl ran completely contrary to his personality, which demanded that any woman he dated be able to bristle with fire as she argued her political point of view, one that he'd oppose, just on basic principle, no matter what it was. As for children, Gil believed in his heart of hearts that kids make great companions—the moment they graduate from law school.

Particular details notwithstanding, Gil is not so different from most people, who tend to view their lives as a still photograph, rather than a movie. Freezing a particular moment in their mind's eye, they embellish the picture into a reflection of whatever they might have heard, been taught, or imagined true happiness to be, while ignoring the changing nature of their complete selves. What they don't want to face is that the notion of an ideal relationship and the actual relationship are two completely different entities. Not surprisingly, when I ask people what kind of person they want as a mate and what plan of action they've developed to find that person, I usually find that they haven't given the problem any careful thought at all. They want only a cardboard fantasy and are waiting for someone else to come along and introduce them to that fantasy.

In essence, these people are deceiving themselves. It's easy to blame everyone and everything else for their inability to find a mate(s). The fact is, they have never really looked. They are, obviously, not serious about finding a mate. They haven't gotten serious enough about real life mating to separate their fantasies from realities.

How about you? Think of your romantic history; have you always been realistic?

HOW WE FOOL OURSELVES

Self-deception cannot always be ascribed to laziness or other more complex, yet conscious, motivations. Sometimes, in searching for a mate, as in all endeavors, there are internal and often unconscious policies that affect our choices and decision making.

The human psyche is a mysterious and vexing power. For many psychological causes, some past forgotten trauma, perhaps, or a stern and disapproving parent, the unconscious mind may sabotage the best intentions of the conscious mind. You believe, on a conscious level, that you're serious about finding a mate, but on a deeper level contrary forces may be subverting that aim.

At birth, a child is intimately connected to the mother, deriving sustenance, nurturing, life itself, from that bonding. A sense of comfort is equated, thereafter, with connectedness. Only gradually does the child learn to separate from the parent. This separation can be assisted and eased, or it can be discouraged and made confusing by the child's parents, depending on their interaction. Children whose parents seem remote may learn to be prematurely separate. They sense early that intimate behavior is unacceptable. But not being acceptable certainly doesn't lessen the need for intimacy. For such children, the thought of intimacy, while held out as a distant ideal, will be fraught with anxiety all their lives, or until the source of the anxiety is examined. While, as adults, they may believe that intimacy is what they want from a mate, their fear of potential rejection and their ancient forgotten memories of real rejection cause them to contrive an infinite number of methods to avoid it. They fall in love with the idea of being in love, but when love's often harsh realities get too close, they find ways to avoid the contact.

You're probably familiar with the psychological agenda of a fat person who has developed a layer of insulation against the world; despite his or her best conscious intentions to diet, the weight remains as protection against emotional intrusion. Then there's the infamous and ubiquitous headache, which provides a sexual partner a ready out from having to perform. Other psychosomatic ailments may be more severe, depending on the importance of the event or relationship to be avoided.

Even more cunningly, your mind may invent some incredibly imaginative arguments why you should not pursue a relationship with this wonderful person whom you have just met or are getting to know. The justifications feel and seem so real that you don't question their validity. Tarnishing makes it easier to justify your dumping that person. You may even believe that person is exactly what you want and need, when something more powerful on a deeper level happens to subvert your happiness.

I once knew a woman who was engaged to a man with whom she was truly compatible, only to break it off because he pronounced the word onion "oonyon." If it hadn't been onion, it would have been something else; she clearly wasn't ready to marry but couldn't face the reality and had to invent an excuse which, no matter how lame, felt critically important.

Now recount again your romantic past. How many lame excuses have you invented, either to break off a relationship or to avoid one completely, or even to rationalize being dumped? How serious were you then? How serious are you now? How much more realistic have you become? What, if anything, did you learn from your relationships?

If you're like most people, you've never given any thought to these questions. You may have even conveniently summed up your feelings beneath a wall of "I'm misunderstood." Rather than seek to clear up the misunderstandings, you believe that romances are "meant to be" or they're not. "If they can't tell who I am, then screw 'em," is the attitude.

But how many times have you given someone who was a real jerk a second chance after the first meeting? And how often have you exhibited that "screw 'em" attitude, only to wonder the next day why you didn't meet someone or were considered arrogant by the person you wanted to meet? First impressions are important, particularly when a bad first impression, inadvertent or not, erases one more person from a list of possibilities.

If you're really serious about finding a mate, your dress, demeanor and speech must all be compatible with your goal. Underneath your rough exterior may indeed lie a sensitive soul waiting to be noticed, but, except for magic or extra sensory perception, how could anyone know that? Underneath your shy exterior may lie the heart of a panther, but who could be expected to divine that information?

The Stranger Across a Crowded Room syndrome just doesn't work in reality, at least, not often enough to rely on it. And knowing intellectually that such predestined arrangements aren't likely to produce results, and going ahead anyway, proves a lack of seriousness. Again, it's the child holding out, waiting for the background music to crescendo and the curtains to part.

You'd probably never consider allowing a child to make important decisions for you, yet that's precisely what you do each time the unconscious past, with its fears of failure and rejection, memories of loss and pain, confounds your best intentions to move forward. A traumatized child grows into an adult whose emotional responses have been blueprinted. Unless realized or re-experienced as a sense of completion, these traumas will continue to tether you to past patterns.

How early experiences and unconscious beliefs can affect what we do today is illustrated by a Great Dane belonging to a patient of mine. This dog is so enormous, he can easily place his paws on top of your head. Nonetheless, when my patient wants to keep him confined to one room of his house, he places on the doorway floor a one-foot high barrier. Now obviously the dog could walk right over this puny wall without breaking stride, but because the same barrier seemed so unfathomably large to the dog when he was a puppy, he never questions it and submits meekly; in his mind, the barrier still towers over him.

In much the same way, human beings can be subverted. With so many of us being ruled by the child within, the fear of intimacy sometimes seems to be as common as the cold. It is, after all, worlds easier to go through a series of superficial relationships than to struggle with a single one that takes commitment, caring and work. (For a much more detailed discussion of intimacy, see Chapter Eight.)

In the past, such anti-intimate behavior has been associated most often with men. Sometimes referred to as the "Peter Pan Principle," it implies that men refuse to grow up, to lose any of their autonomy or freedom. It means that they see intimacy as restrictive, rather than enhancing, as something to fear, rather than cherish. While they may pay lip service to intimacy, even exalting it as the highest virtue, when push comes to shove, these men avoid it as they would prison.

Today, for well-documented sociological reasons, the fear of lost independence applies equally to women, who may mask their fears by appearing to search for the perfect mate. Realistic? Hardly. Inasmuch as no one will ever match their high standards, such women are safe from having to make a commitment. Nowadays, with so much emphasis on exercise and health and beauty, people think of perfection as an absolute standard, a goal that can, in fact, be achieved. So they keep trying, and spend their lives alone.

Blake Edwards, in his film *10*, parodied that conceptual belief by having his protagonist, Dudley Moore, fantasize about a gorgeous woman, a ten, whom he sees on the beach while on vacation alone in Mexico. This beauty, Bo Derek, begins to inhabit his thoughts constantly, haunting him, making him think that if he could ever have her, his life would be complete. Finally, when a twist of fate enables him to realize his goal, the reality renders him apathetic. The so-called ten becomes nothing more than a one-dimensional stick figure, uninteresting and incompatible.

The irony is that so many people fail to understand the film's essential point: there is no perfect "10." The word itself, perfect, is incomplete; perfect for what, or for whom? we must ask. Again, using the analogy of a house, picture a mountain cabin you might once have rented for a short vacation. After a perfectly wonderful time, you may have thought about what a perfect dream house it would be to live in all the time. So you investigated. What you found was that it was a perfect rental house, but as a permanent house it had too many flaws: it needed a new roof, windproofing, insulation, heating system, structural work, and all the rest. Not only that, but evaluating the cabin seriously for full-time habitation made you realize that it was too small, too isolated and too dangerous. So what was a perfect weekend cabin became, on examination, an imperfect full-time residence.

For a more graphic and immediate example, look, if you can, at some photographs taken from the 1940s, 1950s and 1960s of what were then considered to be beautiful women, including Marilyn Monroe. What you will see is that women of those eras had bodies that would be considered *zaftig*, at best, by today's standards.

Like any form of perfection, perfect beauty is an illusion, a changing ideal that flows and ebbs with the times. In the 1980s, it has become acceptable, even desirable, for women through bodybuilding, to build musculature like a man's. This is the only time in recorded history when that has been so, and we are likely, perhaps soon, to revert to past conceptions of beauty. Change is the only constant.

There is, nonetheless, a distinction between a perfectionist and striving for perfection; these are two separate ideas. A perfectionist is a neurotic. He or she believes that an absolute standard can be achieved. Of course, reaching it is an impossibility, causing feelings of incompetence, ineptness and failure.

Striving for perfection is a desirable quality, because the emphasis is placed on the process of striving, not the outcome. The process of developing your body, for example, for its own sake, is a pleasurable activity, whereas needing to mold it to conform to some ephemeral ideal brings no satisfaction. Myself, I know that I will never have the perfect relationship with my wife. What I hope is that we will spend the rest of our lives involved in the process of striving to achieve it. (For that matter, I'll never have the perfect body, either.)

The differences are subtle but important, particularly as they relate to finding a mate. There can be joy in striving to find a compatible mate for the person interested in that, but guilt and anxiety await the perfectionist who feels that every date must measure up to a given code. No date ever will, and no one will ever be good enough for him or her. Believing in the perfect woman or man eliminates you from the ranks of the serious mate hunters.

Now, taking carefully into account all these issues, your fantasies and your reality, the amount of time you've actively spent or are willing to spend to find a mate, the excuses you've manufactured to explain broken relationships, the occasions you were arrogant and felt misunderstood, your fear of intimacy, you search for so-called perfection, ask yourself again: How serious am I?

Discovering You

The way people think about themselves and the perception others have of them rarely coincide exactly. Evaluating ourselves objectively is infinitely more complex than evaluating others. The bank teller you yelled at yesterday for being an incompetent nitwit after he botched up your transaction probably thought you were a hotheaded boob. Who is right, you or the bank teller? Your friend who accompanied you to the bank may have thought you completely justified in getting visibly angry, while the teller's colleagues may have marked you for future reference as someone who's crazy and should be avoided.

IT BEGINS WITH SELF-AWARENESS

In life and relationships, there are no final arbiters of truth, only compromises and subjective value judgments. Are you, in reality, the person you believe yourself to be or the sum total of everyone else's perceptions of you? The truth probably lies somewhere between the two extremes, which vary in distance from person to person.

Those whose relationships are most satisfying and fulfilling have usually narrowed the gap through self-awareness and a willingness to see themselves as others see them. Whether or not they agree with the assessments, they generally remain aware of the impact their actions have on others.

Movie stars who become self-important and narcissistic are said to believe their own press clippings. This sarcastic and biting epigram refers to people who have grown out-of-touch. Most often, their talent, celebrity status and even charisma allow them to attract a steady stream of admirers, yet their relationships are often shallow and one-dimensional.

Do you remember the fable about the insufferably arrogant emperor who wanted to wear only the finest vestments? After being convinced that two visiting tailors had manufactured an outfit unparalleled in the kingdom, but visible only to the wise, he strutted proudly before his subjects wearing only his underwear.

How many of your own press clippings do you believe? How much of what you imagine yourself to be is as genuine as the emperor's new clothes? Are the messages you transmit the ones you want to represent you? How different is your self-image from the image others hold of you? If you were to write a newspaper advertisement honestly listing your dominant personality characteristics, would it be similar to the one your friends would compose about you?

The process of assembling an accurate portrait, taking a self-inventory, of the way you are perceived by others is critically important for anyone wishing to find a mate. If you aren't aware of how you appear to others, your chances of meeting someone with whom you are compatible are probably zilch. Just as you do not usually recognize your own tape-recorded voice (because the sound is coming toward you, not moving away), it may surprise you to discover that your social persona is turning off the very people you'd like to attract, and turning on those you'd like to avoid. You are aware of your personality, the way it feels inside you, but you are not aware of how it impacts others.

By increasing your self-knowledge, you improve, not only your prospects for finding a mate, but the possibility of maintaining the quality of your relationship(s). Houses, cars and stereos don't care a whit about our personalities when we shop for them, but people do.

A COMPOSITE PORTRAIT

Taking a self-inventory may or may not be fun, but it is bound to be enlightening. I have had people tell me that their self images were transformed by the process, so much so that they acquired new confidence and the ability to implement their life plans, both romantic and otherwise, when previously they had been shackled by confusion and self doubts. Whereas before you might have believed you were acting in a vacuum, unaware of the impressions your behavior created, now your actions can be fine-tuned to coincide with your intentions.

A self-inventory requires a realistic approach. You will be drawing a composite portrait of yourself by compiling a list of ten characteristics that you think apply to you, and you will be matching it against the characteristics of the type of mate you would like. If the two do not seem compatible, then you may have some soul-searching to do. Perhaps a reassessment of goals will be necessary, even a reassessment of self. Either way, the extra knowledge gained will serve you in evaluating the reality of your desires.

Then you will be comparing your list against one created by some of your friends or family. It is necessary to enlist people you can trust to be honest in their appraisal of you. Choose people with whom you have relationships that permit dissension and conflicting points of view, no matter how surprising and volatile those revelations may be, without permanent injury, physical or emotional.

A minimum of two other opinions, and a maximum of five, are necessary to give you a consensus of the way you come across to others. Instead of dreading this exercise as a torturous version of *Truth or Consequences*, try to see it as a method by which you and whomever you have chosen can strengthen your relationships through increased bonding. It may even heighten the level of intimacy between you and engender greater communication in the future.

Feeling partly responsible for any progress or success you make due to their efforts, your friends (or family members) will probably make careful and sincere appraisals of you. People love to be invited to participate in other people's lives. Too often their fear of rejection makes them hesitant to initiate that sort of interaction. When a genuine opportunity such as this comes along, most will readily accept the invitation with pleasure and honor. Knowing that they have been chosen to contribute to your life will make your friends feel special. Having this vested interest in your quest to find a mate will make it easier for them later in the program, when you again enlist their assistance.

Make it clear, before they begin work, that you do not want them to write down the characteristics they think you would like to have; such stroking is useless, and even counter-productive to the program. If they are reluctant to be honest, thank them for their forthrightness and find others instead.

Once the assessment begins, nothing may be the same for you again. That sounds melodramatic, and it is. Having the opportunity to view yourself from a point outside your consciousness can be a very sobering experience. The process itself is exciting because the degree of self-knowledge it imparts can be enormous. It may be hard to assimilate much of the information you are given and make some desired changes, but if nothing else, being presented with this list will be an exercise in reality.

The Rules

Below, you will find a rather lengthy list of positive personality characteristics, judged the most common to the greatest number of people, from which you and your friends will compile a "Top Ten." Obviously, not all will apply to everyone, just as some that may be appropriate are not included; if that should be the case, simply add them. This list is provided solely for your ease of use and is not meant to be all inclusive.

Intelligent	Attractive
Good dresser	Modern
Traditional	Liberal
Professional	Business-minded
Serious	Out-going
Playful	Reserved
Sports-minded	Psychologically-minded
Open-minded	Independent
Political	Socially aware
Outdoorsy	Cultural

Domestic	Sexual
Generous	Warm
Athletic	Affectionate
Neat	Honest
Understanding	Financially successful
Funny	Comforting

Discovering Your Top Ten Characteristics

1. In compiling your personality list, choose the top ten characteristics that best describe you. Score yourself from one to ten points on how strong you are on each characteristic. Then add up the numbers to get a total score.

Most people have never really tried to analyze themselves, so thinking clearly about the components of your personality may seem hard. Stay with it and, above all, be honest.

Important: Do not look at any of the lists compiled by your friends before all of them are complete; doing so might influence either you or them.

Here's how *your self-inventory* might look:

1. Your Top Ten:

Characteristic	Rating
1. Intelligent	9
2. Attractive	8
3. Good dresser	9
4. Athletic	8
5. Honest	10
6. Successful	10
7. Sexual	10

8. Funny	10		
9. Political	7		
10. Modest	10	total:	91

Comment: You've given yourself a score of 91, which means that you think pretty highly of yourself.

2. Have your friends rate you from one to ten on each of the characteristics you selected for yourself. No matter how many significant others you choose to ask, do not allow them to show each other their ratings.

Some people who participated in this process made it a game, everyone rating everyone else, regardless of whether they were interested in mating. One woman told me that she and her friends made lists as a party game.

Let's see if *your friends* agree with your self-assessment.

2. A friend's assessment on your Top Ten:

Characteristic	Rating		
1. Intelligent	4		
2. Attractive	7		
3. Good dresser	6		
4. Athletic	2		
5. Honest	10		
6. Successful	9		
7. Sexual	3		
8. Funny	2		
9. Political	10		
10. Modest	10	total:	54

Comment: From your friend's list we've learned that there's a major discrepancy between how you and your friend sees you on your Top Ten. You see yourself as highly intelligent while your friend sees you as low average; you see yourself as a dynamite dresser while your friend says high average; and though you see yourself as athletic, your friend sees you as a couch potato. Now, when it comes to sex you have rated yourself a perfect 10, while your friend sees you as below average, and you see yourself as a comedian while your friend says you are a dud. And lastly, while you walk around thinking you're modest, your friend says you have virtually no modesty at all.

You should now ask yourself why this discrepancy exists. Does it mean that your self-perception is utterly mistaken? Could it mean that your friend doesn't know you? Or could it be that you aren't being honest with yourself? Before rushing to judgment, study the rest of the data.

3. Have your friends compile their own lists of your top ten personality characteristics using the same 1-10 system.

Here is an illustration of what a friend's version(s) of your Top Ten characteristics might look like:

Characteristic	Rating
1. Honest	10
2. Modern	8
3. Professional	9
4. Seriousus	9
5. Political	7
6. Reserved	9
7. Independent	10

8. Understanding	7		
9. Strong	9		
10. Sincere	9	total:	88

Comment: A score of 88 is pretty good. However, the top ten traits your friend sees don't seem to describe the same person you think of yourself as being. Which is the real you? It's possible that both are the real you, that the person you described may be the inner you, while the person your friend described may be your social you, how you appear to the world. Just like the sound of your voice on a tape recorder, the image you project may differ from the one you think you're projecting. This is valuable self-knowledge.

Positive *and* Negative Characteristics

4. Next make up a list of personality characteristics, *both* positive and negative traits, that best describe you.

Your complete list of characteristics, both positive and negative might look like this:

1. Intelligent
2. Attractive
3. Political
4. Funny
5. Honest
6. Impatient
7. Self-righteous
8. Argumentative
9. Self-centered
10. Spoiled

Comment: Your ability to view both your good points and less attractive ones is admirable. To gain a more complete view, though, compare it to the following list.

5. Have your friend also make up a general list that s/he thinks would best describe you, using both positive and negative adjectives.

Your friend's complete list of both positive and negative top ten characteristics, looks like this:

1. Pompous
2. Honest
3. Smart
4. Sarcastic
5. Egotistical
6. Overbearing
7. Demanding
8. Charming
9. Principled
10. Knowledgeable

6. Compare your own list of positive and negative personality characteristics against your friend's lists, noting any major discrepancies.

Comment: For the most part, allowing for language differences, the previous two lists matched well. Your public image and your friends' image of the way you present yourself to the world, as we learned from the first two lists, are quite dissimilar. You present yourself to the world, or think you present yourself to the world, in a particular way. When you asked your friend to evaluate what s/he see as you, you found that she did not see you the same way. On the other hand, when you presented your real self to your friend, you found that she saw you very similarly to the way you saw yourself. Thus, both of you know the real you but see the social you differently.

Now, what should you have learned from these exercises? You have learned: (1) your strengths and weaknesses, as seen through the eyes of others; (2) the discrepancies between your own self-image and the one others have of you; and (3) the areas you must strengthen in order to convey the message you want to convey. If you have several friends participate in this exercise, you may get many different perceptions of you. If that happens, you might want to question the consistency of your behavior: Are you acting a certain way depending on who you're with?

USING WHAT YOU'VE LEARNED

Knowing exactly who you are is useless unless you are willing to look realistically at the type of person with whom you have a reasonable chance of developing a romance. So to meet the type of person (people) you want to meet, use what you've learned about yourself to develop a profile of that person which will realistically align with your own profile. Whom you are looking for depends, obviously, on who you are—hence, the personal inventory. To say you're going after Mel Gibson (or Christie Brinkley) when your personal inventory reveals that you're more like Bette Midler (or Danny De Vito), means that you're not being realistic. While such pairings aren't impossible—indeed, opposites do sometimes attract—the point of this program is to increase your mating probabilities. Disregarding the findings from your personal inventory will decrease the probability of you finding a mate.

Not every date is necessarily a potential permanent mate, even though permanence is a quality most people think of when seeking romance. What usually happens in the dating and mating game is we tend to feel that we have to evaluate whether this certain someone, with whom only a single day or evening has been spent, will make a good wife or husband. We use minimal information to arrive at a major conclusion. In reality, the quest for a permanent mate is a gradual sequence: playmate, friend, roommate, permanent mate, and each of these has its own characteristics. Whether or not you follow this sequence to the letter, the evaluation process actually follows such a pattern before one is comfortable saying "I do."

So take your time; stop to have some fun along the way. If you are happy with someone as a playmate and friend, but find that he or she is, or would seem to be, a terrible roommate, know that permanence is unlikely. Does that mean you should throw away this person with whom you've been having a great time? No, not if you're willing to accept the relationship on its own terms and limitations. You can still have a great time, even if you don't get married.

Different Types of Relationships

There are, in fact, various types of relationships you might be seeking in addition to, or even to the exclusion of, a permanent mate:

- a one night stand—almost always sexual in nature.
- a playmate—someone to have fun with; dancing, skating, drinking, making love, etc.
- a conversationalist—to discuss light and/or serious topics.

- a sports partner——either to play or watch sports with.
- a roommate——of the nonromantic type.

Obviously, there are different criteria for each category, and they do not always translate directly from one to another. Your dancing partner and you may have a terrific time hitting the folk clubs on Tuesday nights, but as a conversationalist, he couldn't describe the difference between irony and iron ore. Your sexual playmate may provide great pleasure, but from the look of the debris in her apartment, she would make a terrible roommate. And so on.

Permanent mates differ from the above specialized categories in that they have the ability to straddle categories. The phrase, "Jack of all trades, master of none," describes the essence of someone with whom you have a reasonable chance of finding emotional, intellectual, physical and even spiritual congruence, the opportunity to achieve permanence. A permanent mate can be a playmate, a business partner, a roommate, a lover, a sports partner.

THE "COMPLETE RELATIONSHIP" MISTAKE

Do not make the mistake, however, of believing that a permanent mate precludes the need for the other types of mates noted above. No one person can satisfy every need of a permanent mate. Nonetheless, many people keep trying to find "the complete relationship"——the someone who can cook, clean, build, earn, play, screw, converse, sympathize, navigate, preach, pray, teach and learn. Such is not the criteria for deciding whether a prospect qualifies for marriage, or some other form of permanence. The more stress placed on the primary relationship, expecting your mate to paint every corner and fill every crack, the higher the probability that fractures will occur. Not even Superman could be all things to Lois Lane.

In reality, the happiest marriages are between partners who know themselves and respect each other well enough to understand that various needs can be met only by a variety of special others. While I am happily married and love my wife dearly, I still have other friends with whom I do things she and I could never share on the same level. With one friend, I play basketball, with another tennis; a third friend and I shoot the bull over a few beers, and yet another friend and I get together periodically to speak philosophically, whether of Washingtonian politics or the politics of the soul.

My wife similarly has a bevy of friends and acquaintances with whom she: shops, talks, plays and entertains. What allows us to continually nourish our relationship together is the complete acceptance of the fact that we are not compatible every hour of every day.

I want you now to prepare a preferred characteristic list for each of the following categories: permanent mate, roommate, friend, playmate. Of course, you will see some overlap between them all, as well as some distinct differences. While their relative rankings will change as you change, the point is to provide you with a list that will aid your understanding of their basic differences, as well as your priorities in each category.

The following is a list I drew up several years ago for myself; it is presented only as a sample, and is not meant to influence your choices except by illustration:

PLAYMATE	FRIEND	ROOMMATE	PERMANENT
sexy	intelligent	responsible	sexy
attractive	fun-loving	organized	intelligent
fun-loving	warm	neat	responsible
spontaneous	loving	intelligent	funny
adventurous	funny	tolerant	warm
outdoorsy	understanding	considerate	understanding
sensuous	loyal	funny	loyal
warm	responsible	warm	attractive
loving	open	understanding	open
understanding	compatible	compatible	sensuous

As you can see from this example, there is considerable overlap between the four categories, but the order of preference is significantly different.

The interesting thing about compiling this list is that, in the process of evaluating your preferences, you may in fact discover that the person you thought you wanted to meet is a playmate, or a combination or succession of dates/mates, not a permanent mate. I have seen it happen countless times: after taking the self-inventory, believing the intent was to find a permanent mate, the person discovers that permanence was not the goal at all.

Most people believe that the message they must give to the world is: "I am in the market for a permanent mate, a marriage partner." In truth, however, many really are not and end up living a lie. Permanent relationships may not suit every personality, and connubial "bliss" isn't possible for every citizen, no matter what the magazines say. Just because someone doesn't care to invest the time, trouble, and emotion in a permanent relationship doesn't mean that he or she is afraid of intimacy or reluctant to grow up. Very often, extremely ambitious people, who want to devote themselves completely to their art or commerce, live lives outside their work devoid of intimate human contact. And that's how they prefer it; to do otherwise would only be a charade, and ultimately self-defeating.

For men, the tendency to pretend that marriage is the ultimate goal may arise out of a need to prove that they have souls and depth, because that's what is expected of them. For women, the motive may be to show their parents, family or friends that they aren't loose.

Single life is unquestionably a viable alternative to marriage for a large portion of the population. No matter what others may say about your decision not to settle down right now, and no matter what your parents taught you about meeting the right mate, and no matter what some radio psychologist told you about your failure to meet Mr. or Ms. Right, being single is your God-given right.

In this book, in speaking of finding a mate, I am referring only to the kind of mate appropriate to your aims, whatever they may be. Although the majority of the population seems to be searching for a permanent mate, that doesn't mean the same goal necessarily applies to you, too. At least not right now. Who you are and what you desire may fluctuate at various times in your life, and satisfying each need requires a different approach.

For people who cannot, or do not want to, abide by the constrictions inherent in a permanent one-on-one relationship, a succession of specialized playmates is a perfectly acceptable alternative. One woman who did the program had tossed away dozens of men in the past because they hadn't satisfied her apparent desire for a jack-of-all-trades. Yet these men were wonderful playmates who, had she known previously what she learned through the self-inventory, would have made perfect additions to a stable of dates designed to satisfy different needs or moods.

It makes no difference to me, and is no business of anyone else, the kind of person you choose to be or the mate(s) or dates you choose to pursue. The point of this program is to help you understand first what your true goals are, and then provide you a plan of action to realize them. Allowing you to realize your personal goals in terms of mating, from the kinky to the mundane, is the purpose of this book.

Remember: the connection between two people is for no one, not me, not anyone, but those two to judge.

Keeping both that information in mind and the results of your own self-inventory, now compile your four potential dates/mates lists.

After you're fairly certain that each list accurately reflects your criteria for that type of person, think of friends, roommates, playmates, and permanent mates that you have had in the past or have now. Rank each of them, using the 1-10 scale, against your master list. If, for example, the friends you listed are current friends, their scores should be fairly high; conversely, failed friends or past romantic partners probably received relatively low scores, or at least low scores in certain key areas. A friend who scores zero on loyalty, despite getting nines in other categories, is not likely to be a very good friend. Going through this process can yield valuable insights into yourself and your relationships.

Assuming Power

Where is the best place to find a mate? Everywhere.

Opportunity occurs where you find it, and where you find it should be wherever you are. Successful mating is a state of mind, not a matter of luck or timing. It is a state of mind that can be learned.

A WORLD OF SOCAL CONTACTS

People who attract an unending stream of potential dates and mates do not mentally segregate good places from bad places. To them, the world is one big singles bar, with some possibilities more possible than others. The dentist's office, the muffler shop, a book store, everyplace they go, they keep their eyes open, alert. Instead of staring straight ahead in the supermarket, they look at others; they strike up conversations; they're friendly.

They like people.

What they don't believe is that social contacts can be made only in assigned social situations. And out of their fondness for people——even just saying hello to strangers ——they meet mates.

As you must already know, I'm not advocating that you simply attack willy-nilly, without regard to the type of person you really want as a mate. What I am implying is that you can learn from other people every day by simply noticing their tendency to make themselves available.

That's all.

Mating should be a top priority in your life (it probably already is, otherwise you wouldn't be reading this book). Your mission, as you follow my program, is to find prospects, whether they be potential life mates, dates, or perfect playmates. Attaining a mating consciousness will enable you to carry out successfully some form of this program every place you go, in everything you do.

Every situation must be viewed as a possibility, an opportunity. The thought you should hold constantly is: "How does this fit into my plan?"

By that I don't mean you have to be actively hunting when you, say, pick up a newspaper from the corner vendor. But I do want you to understand that the realization of your goal rests on your changing the way you think.

I want you to discard all your prior beliefs about where to go to find mates and dates, and, until your goal is met, keep your awareness level high in places whose romantic potential you formerly ignored.

The Little Things You Do

Smile at people; ask them how they are. At first, it doesn't even matter whether you feel they could be potential mates—or even whether they are of the opposite sex. Simply get in the practice of putting yourself out there.

In the smallest ways, from raking the lawn and smiling at a passersby, to doing your laundry at the laundromat and offering to help someone carry a big load, making yourself available to people will ultimately help you notice the zillions of possibilities you have missed in the past. That goes for your job, too.

You don't have to say hello only to those to whom you're attracted. Get in the habit of greeting, or visually acknowledging with a nod of the head or a smile, whoever might pass, whether old or young. Because as you begin to make contact with the world at large, the mating process itself becomes easier.

Assuming power—seizing it—is what this section of the program is all about. With most of us living in our own isolated shells, a simple hello, a gesture made without waiting for the other person to initiate contact, conveys the impression that you are powerful—because you are the one who has broken the egg; you are the one who has shattered the silence.

The most frequently absurd situation we face socially is the elevator in which passengers stare blankly either at their feet or the floor indicator lights. I say absurd not because the situation itself is inherently so, but because we have turned the intimacy of the elevator into something that induces almost painful self-awareness in many people. Yet whenever one brave soul strikes up conversations with his fellow passengers, the sense of relief everyone else feels is almost palpable. They respond, most often, instantly and enthusiastically to his overtures. His unashamed friendliness gives him an aura of power.

I have often struck up conversations with other drivers while inching along in traffic. With the road more resembling a parking lot than the freeway, I yell some comment to the nearest driver which indicates how annoying traffic jams can be, and almost every time, my overture is met with surprising friendliness and acceptance.

Even if your overtures are made only to nonthreatening old ladies, a sense of power accumulates in you, a feeling of sociability becomes embedded. Eventually, your entire outlook will be brightened, your ease of romantic contact improved. Just as an actor must practice his technique, so, too, must you learn to convey joy and warmth through your greetings.

Take the time to say hello to at least five people everyday. If you can, strike up conversations. They don't have to be about anything in particular, nor do they need to be of any particular length. Talking briefly about the weather is fine.

Of course, it's easiest to converse with strangers when we share something in common. People from New York, for example, whose accents identify them instantly, will, in other cities, strike up spontaneous conversations, if not friendships, because of that common bond. Ironically, as New Yorkers, they probably wouldn't have given each other the time of day if they were back home.

A friend of mine, who regularly dates many different types of men, meets them as she walks her dog. Actually, she doesn't even own a dog, nor does she particularly like them. Yet she knows that dog owners always have something to talk about, a safe topic that easily breaks the ice. So she carries a leash with her wherever she goes. When she sees an attractive man walking his dog, she pulls out her leash and approaches him, asking whether he's seen her golden retriever anywhere. Only rarely does the man ever catch on to her scheme, and even when he does, contact has been made, and he's usually flattered.

Once when we were shopping together, she saw a man who appealed to her walking his dog. Lacking the confidence to approach him without the leash, she ran back to the car to get it, then ran to catch up with him to ask if he'd seen her dog. The last I saw of her that day was as she, the man, his dog, and her leash all disappeared up the street, together.

PERFECT LABORATORIES

Bars, clubs, parties, dances, mixers, supermarkets, singles functions—they're all potential mating grounds. And, believe it or not, each has its own particular function and usefulness in your program, whether you're looking for a life mate or a playmate.

Those who are shy or intimidated or elitist tend to believe bars are beneath them; others view them as the next thing to a whorehouse. But for our purposes here, bars are wonderful laboratories for social experimentation.

The very facelessness of a bar, its anonymity, offers opportunities unavailable anywhere else. For example, if you want to practice talking casually to someone, in preparation for more serious conversations when the time comes, bars are unequalled. Why? Because the likelihood of ever seeing that same person there again, or being recognized by anyone who knows you already, is small, so you are free to be as outrageous as you want.

Exploring the Boundaries of Self

At a Halloween party one often assumes the personality dictated by a mask and costume. In the same way, bars offer a disguise; they enable you to practice different personas and different methods of relating. You can strike up conversations with other people in order to decide which opener is superior. You can change your clothing, affect new mannerisms, even modify enunciation. If you'd like, you can alter completely your identity for the evening and have fun playing someone else.

Certainly, I'm not advocating that you undergo a personality transplant. But as we discovered in the self-inventory, you may really have several different personas, depending on the company and locale. By practicing your skills, you will be able to call upon the one you want when you want it. To be successful socially one must be able to implement an array of skills and behaviors appropriate both to the situation and the person. Just as you wouldn't put your feet up on the desk and tell bawdy jokes when interviewing with the President for a job in his cabinet, you'd probably want to assume different airs of sophistication when meeting Princess Diana and Cyndi Lauper. That doesn't mean you've changed you, it means you've adapted appropriately.

Cary Grant, perhaps the Twentieth Century's epitome of cool sophistication, was born Archibald Alexander Leach to a poor English family which could offer him none of the upper-class privileges he wanted. As a young man, Archie's fantasy was to live the type of elegant life he read about in books. So he pretended, practicing a proper Oxford accent, dressing the part, acting the role the way he visualized it. And eventually, Archibald Leach, the actor, actually became Cary Grant, the man he had once pretended to be.

Bars offer the perfect vehicle for experimenting with personas, especially if you discovered during your self-inventory that your self-concept and the image you present to others do not match. For example, a man who has dressed his entire life in corduroys and loafers and has learned, through the self-inventory, that he is presenting himself in a way that is contrary to his goals, would have difficulty suddenly changing attire around his friends; they may ridicule or criticize his attempts to break out of the mold, which, in a sense, has defined his personality. At a bar, he could, if he wished, put on a lame jumpsuit and sequined shoes, pretending to be the kind of person who wears those things. If it feels right and he likes the results, he may even want to adopt that style. After experiencing some success with his new duds, he will undoubtedly feel more comfortable telling his friends to bug off.

Whether or not you need or want to develop some sort of alter-ego, bars are terrific for meeting playmates and one-nighters and developing communication skills, in other words, small talk. Some people report that they worked best to that end when they became regulars at a particular bar.

Being a regular gives you a sense of purpose, a sense of confidence, when you walk in. Think of the camaraderie developed by the characters in the television series *Cheers*. Because people are at their best when they're most relaxed, feeling at home in a bar allows you to pretend that anyone you might meet there is, in a sense, visiting your home.

Get to know the bartenders and waiters/waitresses. Naturally, if you leave a somewhat hefty tip the first time, you'll make a positive impression. Then return on successive nights; if you space your visits out too far apart, you're likely to be forgotten. Three visits spaced closely together are better than a dozen spread out over a year.

Incidentally, you don't have to drink yourself silly every night. In fact, getting loaded when trying to meet people, might remove some of your inhibitions, but it is counterproductive to your aims. No one likes a staggering drunk, except another staggering drunk.

When the personnel get to know you, they will be able to introduce you to other regulars and newcomers. In effect, they'll become your agents. Bartenders, waiters and waitresses love to act as matchmakers, and having them play that role makes any introduction easier. They could, for example, arrange an accidental meeting; they could tell whomever you happen to be interested in what a great person you are.

A client of mine became a regular at a neighborhood bar by attending every Monday night during the football season to watch Monday Night Football games. Week after week, when he walked in, there would be other people who recognized him. Soon, he developed acquaintances and a few friendships with the other regulars, and a whole new network of possibilities was opened to him. It happened more quickly for my friend because there was a common thread, a shared experience, that bound them all: the football game.

Each bar has its own personality, hence, its own purpose in your program. Some bars are noted for being pick-up joints; others may be good for conducting informal business meetings; others are for gays only; some are for locals; some cater to out-of-town clientele. They also have their own particular, sometimes peculiar, style: down home, blue collar, yuppie, trendy, affluent, funky, and so on.

Of course, not every bar may be suitable to your aims. If, for example, you walk into a bar and there are men dancing cheek to cheek, but you're looking for someone a little straighter, then choose some other place. If you decide a fun and frivolous playmate is your current priority, and the bar you've chosen suggests something members of British Parliament might frequent, then you've made an incorrect choice. Conversely, if you'd like to meet a professional person, someone with a disciplined lifestyle, and you walk into a bar where the music is blasting at 1,000 decibels, then another locale is probably more appropriate.

All of which is certainly not to imply a straight person can't be found in a gay bar, a playmate in a staid bar or a serious business person in a raucous bar, but you may safely assume that the odds favor finding them in places where, stereotypically, that person is more likely to be found.

You've wasted enough time in the past, waiting for romance to find you, so now use your time to best advantage. Go to places where the chances of finding your targeted personality are high. To test an alternative persona (or not), choose bars which enable you to practice your social skills and yield a potential mate. There are, after all, only twenty-four hours in a day, and if you can consolidate tasks, do so. Always rember your personal goal.

Of course, your short-term goal may differ from day to day, depending on your mood. On Tuesday you may feel the urge to search for a permanent mate; on Friday you may feel that you want someone to play with, and nothing more.

Many people have had great success matching a particular bar to their particular goal—Bar X for watching sports, Bar Y for meeting playmates, Bar Z for locating an ideal permanent mate—by compiling a sort of bar guide.

Think of yourself as an investigative reporter whose job it is to critique different bars: the names and brief personality descriptions of the employees, the type of bar (trendy, blue collar, and so forth), its hours of operation, activities or games played there, ambiance, whether the crowd changes according to the time of night, the parking situation, any entertainment—everything you ever wanted to know about a bar should be included.

Not only will this guide prove valuable in the future when you want to meet a specific personality, the actual compilation of it (writing down the information in a notebook) will allow you to feel comfortable walking into any bar, because you have a particular assignment: not to meet anyone, necessarily, but to collect information. Ironically, while you are not trying to meet someone, you may very well do so, because a person performing a task is almost always more intriguing than one sitting idly.

No matter what happens you can't lose when compiling the bar guide. If you do make contact, terrific; if you don't, at the very least you've done your homework, obtained some useful information and advanced in the program.

Eventually, you will become comfortable going out without having to make notes in the bar guide as a crutch. Its purpose then will be simply to refresh your memory, enabling you to match your mood and intention to locale.

RATING PARTNERS

Whether looking for a permanent mate or a playmate, always know exactly the characteristics you prefer in that particular person. As we already discussed, the most important characteristics of a friend, a roommate, a permanent mate and a playmate differ significantly, and it's up to you to use the information you have to decide whether or not a particular person conforms to your target. Why waste your time with anyone less? Knowing exactly what your criteria are for each will make your job easier, no matter what mood you're in, and help to maximize your time because you'll be able to qualify your efforts.

Here are sample ratings for three people I knew when I was single. Much like the personal inventory, I rated each according to my list of preferred personality characteristics for that specific type of mate: permanent mate, playmate and friend. I am including the chart for you to see because I want you to get in the habit of rating everyone you meet. Study how it works:

Mate	Rating
competent	9
sensual	10
intelligent	9
independent	9
energetic	9
warm	10
introspective	9
understanding	9
funny	10

Total score   94
Conclusion: Perfect Partner

Playmate	Rating
sexual	2
attractive	9
adventurous	3
fun	2
outgoing	4
rich	10

athletic	2
funny	5
affectionate	4

Total score   41
Conclusion: Not for Me

Friend	Rating
understanding	7
loyal	9
considerate	9
reliable	8
good listener	9
warm	7
open	10
sense of humor	8
intelligent	9

Total score   76
Conclusion: Get Friendly

The rating you see in the first column is the one for the woman who eventually became my wife. The second is for someone I decided, based on the final score, to have nothing to do with because I didn't want another empty acquaintance and knew that we could only go so far together. The third is for someone who is still a very good friend.

Don't Waste Time

Just like my friend, who believed it was as easy to fall in love with a wealthy girl as a poor one, you may as well practice your social skills with someone who appears to fit your personality criteria. Don't become involved with people who just do not fit your preference list and are therefore likely to be incompatible.

One of the purposes of listing the characteristics of your ideal mate/mates, besides helping you to crystallize your intentions, is to allow you to focus on what it is you need and want. Rating someone with whom you are interested in pursuing a serious relationship will help you to get a more concrete sense of your potential compatibility. At the same time, knowing your preferred characteristics for a playmate will enable you to decide rather quickly whether this person meets your requirements. For instance, if nonsmoking is the quality you assigned the most weight to, and you find yourself in conversation with someone who lights one cigarette off the last, excuse yourself and move on.

Ignoring such findings may place you in unwanted situations with unwanted people inappropriate to your aims. Believing that mates are scarce, that all the good men and women have been taken, many people latch on to any warm body in the hopes of establishing a relationship, regardless of whether that person is right for them. They disregard the evidence they've been given and develop a mind-set that says, "I'm going to make this work."

Mind-sets

A woman looking for a man who will, above all other things, be faithful to her would be foolish to ignore her first-time date's admission that, at that moment, he's cheating on his wife. So attracted is she to him, she may want to believe that he would never do the same to her, but such a mind-set would doom her to inevitable heart-break. All such mind-sets do.

Consider the outcome of the case of the psychiatrist-in-training who had a similar tendency. He told a female patient of his that he would be unable to see her for two weeks because he was planning to take his vacation. Hearing the news, she replied, "Well, I'm going on vacation for three weeks."

"I'm going across country," he said.

"Well," she said, "I'm going around the world."

"How nice," he said.

"I've got a headache," she said.

"Oh," he said, "would you like some aspirin?"

Hearing him retell this story later, the psychiatrist-in-training's supervisor said to him, "Your patient wasn't really going around the world. Nor did she have a headache. Her responses were her way of telling you how angry she was at you for leaving her for two weeks."

Feeling chagrined and stupid for not interpreting his patient's rechanneled anger, the psychiatrist made another appointment with her before leaving on vacation. When she came in his office, she was terribly distraught, devastated, sobbing uncontrollably.

"My husband and children were just in a car accident," she said. "They're all dead."

In the most sympathetic tone he could muster, the psychiatrist said, "You're really angry I'm going on vacation, aren't you?"

Mind-sets are self-defeating. While you may be tantalized by the possibilities, contorting the other person's personality into your misshapen sense of accommodation, at best, wastes your time; at worst, it breaks your heart. The point of undergoing the analysis and examination of the self-inventory is to save both your time and your heart.

Your self-inventory and ideal mate list allow you to collect an amazing amount of pertinent information in very little time, as long as you are sensitive to the clues people provide. Without that knowledge of who we are and what we need, we spend whole evenings, or days, or possibly years, locked in on the wrong person. Unable to separate your needs and desires from other people's, you probably repeated mistakes, choosing the same person with a different face and name. Each time you were predestined to fail. It was the Spanish-American philosopher George Santayana who said that those who cannot or will not remember the lessons of the past are condemned to repeat them.

Drawing a clear picture of who you are and whom you are looking for, you can avoid making the same mistakes over and over again.

Armed with a strategy, you have the ammunition to use your time wisely. For example, those seeking a partner who can intelligently discuss Hegelian dialectics and the birth of the Neo-Romantic movement in post World War II Yugoslavia would be wise to back away from someone who wants to talk about nothing but the latest informative issue of *TV Guide*. Unless the purpose of the tryst is only quick thrills and chills, the romance is likely to be a bust. Even then, check your playmate preference list. If having an intelligent conversation apres ranks highly, this person is not for you. Don't waste time on someone who doesn't fit your targeted personality profile. Playmates, too, must be compatible in order to be fun.

Certainly, the choice is yours. But undergoing some severe soul-searching, as you did compiling the self-inventory, generally reveals qualities and tendencies that should be heeded. Discarding your findings in favor of chemistry (read: sex) for a permanent mate is likely to lead to a dead end, as you may have discovered.

Not only do I want to help you find a mate (if that is indeed your goal), I also want you to maintain permanence through congruence.

INCREASING YOUR VISIBILITY

Since your intention is to increase the probability of finding a mate by enlarging the pool of eligible possibilities, you must literally go where the action is. That certainly doesn't mean you have to hang out at wild nightspots, but neither can you be a recluse, unless, of course, you join Recluse's Anonymous in order to find someone just like you at a meeting.

Everything you do—or almost everything, I'll leave it to your good taste and sense of discretion to decide which is which—must be done outside your home, where you're visible, where you can see and be seen.

If you like to read, go to the park or the library; most libraries have weekly book discussions at which you can meet other avid readers. If you paint, pay a few dollars to do so at a public studio, or take painting lessons, whether you need them or not. The same is true with dancing, which is a wonderful social activity that does not, at dances themselves, necessarily lead to social contact; a much more interaction-oriented activity is dance lessons, at which students, during breaks, seem to bond quickly when sharing their insecurities over trying to learn the latest steps.

Find ways to make your private moments less private.

Interest Clubs

That said, I want you now to make another list, this
time of all the activities you enjoy doing. Everything. From
cooking and gardening, to analyzing samples of sand and
repairing old tractors. Include activities you may have
done only once or twice in your life but would do more if
you could, like skiing, deep sea fishing and traveling in
(for example) Asia. Even include activities you may have
read about and are intrigued by: mountain climbing,
hot-air ballooning, isolation tank floating. The result
should be an all-inclusive list of activities and interests.

From this list, you are going to try to develop a
network of clubs and activity groups. The idea is that
people are united more easily and naturally by their
shared or common interests than when they are thrown
into a vacuum and expected to relate. Just as that friend
of yours with a reputation for being witty flares his nostrils
and stares blankly into space when someone suddenly
demands that he be funny, no one can be expected to just
perform on cue; this is why blind dates have such a high
rate of disaster.

First, prioritize the interests on your list, ranking them
according to the strength of your interest. Place the
strongest interest activities at the top.

Next, use every resource available to you to find a club
or meeting group whose members share the same interest.
Whether they meet weekly, monthly, or bi-monthly, join
as many of these groups, starting from the top of the list
on down, as your schedule and energy permit. It matters
not at all how big or small the gatherings are. Your
purpose in joining is to be with people who share similar
interests. In fact, it doesn't even matter if the members
are all of your sex, because a resulting friendship might

lead to other possibilities. However, common sense indicates that mixed gender clubs are vastly preferable.

Do you like movies? Join a film club in which the members attend films together and talk about them. It is the discussion that makes the club social, not the movie going itself, which is basically a solitary experience.

Do you like politics? Join a civic club, or work to support a particular candidate of your choosing while getting to know his or her other supporters.

Are you intellectually oriented? Join MENSA, the international club for people with high IQs; or a chess club or computer club; or become a docent at your local museum.

Are you an adventurer? Join a travel club.

Sports? Sailing clubs, racquetball clubs, running, biking, weight-lifting and tennis clubs, as well as softball teams.

A collector? There is literally no end to the number of collectors' clubs, from antiques, coins and cars, to stamps, memorabilia and Coca-Cola mementos.

Whatever interests you have, you can be sure that other people in your area share the same interests. Develop your memberships to reflect your most passionate interests. That way, attending these clubs will be joyful, not boring, and help you to break the mind-set that looking for a mate is a distasteful experience, which is likely the attitude you've always had toward it.

Most people think that shopping for a new hat is more fun than shopping for a mate. Why? Because while shopping can be exciting, browsing, trying things on, comparing and selecting, mate searching is an activity filled with uneasiness, uncertainty and dread. Those attitudes are the ones most mate-hunters have manifested all their lives. "Oh," they say, "I guess I'd better find someone." It's no wonder that the mating search for most people has become comparable, in terms of enjoyment, to a trip to the dentist.

Let's change the way you think about mating. Let's make mating an activity you actually look forward to. In a sense, we can apply similar techniques that behavioral therapists use to cure someone of a bad habit or phobia. By associating the bad habit with a nasty experience, say, nail biting with a nauseating taste, the urge to repeat it is diminished over time. Likewise, associating mating with pleasant pursuits will allow you to enjoy the process.

Discussing killer whales of the Pacific Northwest, if that is your predilection, at the monthly meeting of the local cetacean society may help you find the mate of your dreams. If not, at least you've had a good time. At best, you've had a good time and met someone with whom you share something in common, a good jumping-off point from which to explore the (budding?) relationship.

When you do something you enjoy, you never feel cheated or wish that you'd spent the time more productively. You can have fun and meet and mate.

The truth is, you are always more attractive, more magnetic, when engaged in activities you enjoy. By giving yourself up wholly and completely to the enjoyable activity, it's as if a seductive odor is emitted from your pores. You are relaxed and confident, so it's easier for you to make contact. People want to know you.

Add to that equation another person who's also enjoying the activity and the chances of making serious contact are increased many times over.

Be specific as you compile your list of activities. For example, if you include basketball, does that mean you like to watch basketball or play basketball? If you like to play, then joining a co-ed league would be appropriate. If you like to watch, then going to a game is the ticket for you.

You must realize, though, that attending a game by yourself would be silly, because the chances of meeting another single fan are remote.

No. Your task is to find an already existing group of basketball fans who, drawn together by their love of the sport, attend games *en masse* either to catch a break on group pricing or for the love of companionship. If no existing group can be found, then start one. This can be done in several ways: a newspaper ad in the sports section if you can afford it, announcements on local bulletin boards, or flyers on trees and telephone poles.

These methods work when you need to form any interest or activity group not already existing in your area. The name of the game at this point in the program is action. Whatever you can do to take control of the situation, do it. Your whole life, probably, you have waited passively for someone to come along. Now you must assume control, and that includes becoming the catalyst to form an interest group. Being alone and wishing you weren't will not help you meet anyone. Thinking of dating as an evil necessity will not either. What will help, is being with people.

Looking for a new suit of clothes or a car is pleasurable because the choices literally fill the racks and dealerships. We even take our friends along, asking their advice. But because we believe that potential mates are a scarce commodity that someone else could easily steal, we are reluctant to make the search fun and interesting by going out with our buddies, asking their advice and support. We fear the competition; we fear they may abscond with our best piece of merchandise.

No wonder we sometimes refer to the hunt as the "Saturday night meat (meet?) market."

If, however, we could attack the situation with someone we trust, someone who could say, "You didn't approach that woman the way we talked about in group," or, "Go ahead, just say hello to that man," our mind-set would change, and the situation would instantly become pleasurable and more rewarding.

Where do you find people to do that? In an interest group composed of singles whose purpose is to help each other and encourage each other in pursuit of common goals.

Romance clubs

From objective input, such as the type called for in the personal inventories, to moral support, needed whenever your resolve begins to wane, Romance Clubs provide the necessary medicine.

Now, don't rush to the Yellow Pages and scan the "R" listings for "Romance Clubs," because they don't exist, yet. It's up to you to start one in your area. And while it may be difficult for some of you to gather the courage and initiative necessary to start one, I don't think any of you can fail to see the usefulness of a Romance Club. Furthermore, I don't think Romance Clubs are any more difficult to begin than any other interest club, and in fact may be easier. Any of the techniques, or a combination of them all, described above will almost certainly be successful in attracting other interested singles to a weekly, bi-weekly, or monthly meeting of people interested in the same thing you are: romance. And whether or not you actually date any of the other members or simply rely on each other for support in such activities as the personal inventory, you will be taking giant steps toward your goal.

The first item on a romance club's agenda is introductions. Each member takes a turn providing some personal identification and history, particularly as it relates to dating and explaining their reasons for attending the club.

Second, there is a round of first-impression feedback given by each member to every other member. Feedback is going to be an integral part of the club's methodology; at each meeting, there will be a significant portion of the program devoted to providing individual feedback.

Third, members read their lists of ideal mate characteristics to the others. A subsequent round of discussions may provide the members some clues why they haven't been able, to that point, to find such a person. For instance, "You're not defining an ideal, you're describing a fantasy," might come the response from a member. "You're being unrealistic."

Fourth, each member prepares a list describing the salient characteristics of the other members, whether they're first impressions or insights gained over time.

Fifth, each member presents a self-description—the top ten characteristics (from the self-inventory in Chapter Four).

Sixth, all members take that list and rate the member in each characteristic. "You see yourself as funny, but I only give you a three . . .. You say you're a sharp dresser, but to me you look like a 1960s refugee, so I give you a two."

More than anything, Romance Clubs are support groups, supporting you in pursuit of your goal. Particularly if you are squeamish about asking your friends to assist you with your self-inventory, a Romance Club is a resource, a refuge, you can turn to without fear or embarrassment. For comfort, sympathy, advice, ideas and creative input, Romance Club members are unequalled.

Broken down to its most elemental, the simple reasoning behind joining romance and interest clubs, as well as getting out into places from bars or to libraries, is for you to meet as many people as possible. The more people you know, the greater are your chances of meeting someone with whom you stand a healthy chance of mating. It follows logically, then, that since you can't be in more than one place at a time, your prospects are limited to the amount of activities you can squeeze into the day.

That is, unless you have an agent or agents working on your behalf, someone to be your eyes while your eyes are looking elsewhere.

Your Personal Network

Just as an author needs an agent to sell his work while he's creating further works, so, too, can you profit from a network of friends, relatives, business associates, dentists, doctors, accountants, lawyers, hairdressers, manicurists, clients, anyone with whom you have more than casual contact, to act on your behalf. And you probably won't have to pay them fifteen percent for their trouble.

Anyone can become an agent for you. While you may feel embarrassed at telling such people that you are in the market for a so-and-so type of mate and asking them to watch for someone who fits the bill, the fact is that most everyone likes to play matchmaker.

If, for example, you tell your physician during your annual checkup that you would like him to be on the lookout for you, he may immediately remember that his head nurse is also in the market, for someone, perhaps, just like you.

My accountant just successfully fixed up a client, he told me, with his brother. She had casually mentioned to him that she was exploring all avenues, and that if he happened to know anyone who might be suitable——she gave him a list of qualities important to her——to please let her know. Later that same afternoon, the accountant called her back to describe his single brother. Even though it was in the middle of tax season, the accountant made time for this project. He told me later that he was actually flattered that she thought enough of him to ask his opinion, and he was especially gratified to find out, a few weeks later, that the two of them got along very well.

Dating Services

Of course, the quintessential agenting method is a professional dating service.

Believe me, I'm not unaware of, or unfamiliar with, the reservations you may have about enlisting in a dating service, or, for that matter, accepting any of the advice given here that requires your active participation. The reason my program works is that it increases the likelihood of success by putting control of your dating and mating life into your own hands. It makes you responsible for finding more appropriate mates. Perhaps the reason you haven't yet found a mate is that you have always sat back and waited. Well, obviously, you wouldn't be reading this book if that approach had worked, so why not try something different? It's okay if you lack the confidence to engage in any aspect of the program immediately, just as long as you begin at the beginning; take small steps and proceed slowly. But above all, remember that the program works as long as you do. In this case, though, work can also be play.

Many people seem to have the notion that dating services are strictly for creeps—"only the lonely"—but I believe that they're valuable and can be fun.

Remember, I'm advocating that you let everyone know you're out there, available, and dating services help you prescreen potential mates in a very safe atmosphere. Not only that, they save the busy person a very precious commodity, time. People who are successful often use these services because of their efficiency. Like the decorator who will sort through thousands of rolls of wallpaper to bring you only the four or five he believes you will like, the dating service filters out the applicants judged not to be compatible with you and presents you with only those with whom you are likely to have something, at least, in common.

People who join a dating service take an aggressive stand, proclaiming that they are serious about mating.

The vital statistics sheet used by any dating service will ask many of the same questions I've been asking: your interests, likes, dislikes, idiosyncrasies, and ideal mate characteristics.

These days, many of the better services use videotape to facilitate the process, which helps you in two ways: it shows you your potential dates and allows you to judge for yourself how you come off to others. If you've never seen yourself interviewed on film or tape, the result may shock you and will certainly augment the personal inventory assessment. Between hearing your voice, observing facial expressions and body posture, and interpreting communication skills, you will have, maybe for the first time, an objective experience of you—how others see you.

By the way, if you own a video camera, or have access to one, similar sessions can be extremely helpful in your Romance Club. After you've been interviewed by one of the members, all of you together can critique the tape, deciding where you need bolstering or smoothing. Rather than just relying on other club members' opinions, you will be able to see the evidence for yourself.

Any time a dating service applicant chooses to meet another applicant, the second applicant also has to approve the meeting. That process, too, can provide some important information. Say, for example, that you reject everyone who allegedly fits your criteria. Maybe, then, something is missing from your personal inventory. It would be best to investigate further the source of the discrepancy.

Conversely, if the applicants you're interested in all seem to be saying no to meeting you, that's a trend you need to examine.

Before joining any dating service, do some thorough legwork. Find out how long the company has been in business; how many people have signed up; what is their success rate; will they give you the names of satisfied clients to contact; how many referrals will you get for your initial fee?

In other words, when you use a dating service, apply the same criteria you would in choosing any professional service. Above all, make certain the agency represents the type of person you are looking for.

YOUR JOURNAL

In order to make the program really work for you, it is crucial that you keep a journal, a record of everything you do with regard to the program. Each time you smile at someone, go home and record the date and time and circumstances of the encounter. When you talk to someone, write down the name, date, place it happened and nature of the conversation. Give the name of every person you ask to be your agent. Include every step you take toward joining or starting an interest club or a Romance Club.

As you get further into the program, this diary will allow you to see the progress you make, even when you feel frustrated and want to chuck it all. Counting your successes and moments of enlightenment will give you the impetus to continue. Check for patterns of behavior, places you were comfortable in or met someone, then ask yourself what you've learned since that last time out.

Remember, this entire process takes work. It is a not a matter of just sitting idly, waiting, as before, for Mr. or Ms. Right to fall out of the attic. No, it takes days of actually, actively, getting out there and . . . working.

It is the program in its entirety that makes it effective, not selecting bits and pieces that appeal most to you. That means you have to do it all: adopt an open attitude; stick to the findings of the personal inventory and desired mate lists; form Romance Clubs; practice your social skills in bars and lounges and other locations where people congregate; attend classes and lectures; tell your friends and professional acquaintances what you're after.

STICKING WITH YOUR STRATEGY

Above all, have patience. Don't hopscotch steps, hoping to get the rewards any faster; believe me, that doesn't work. This program doesn't succeed by your cherry picking the items that appeal to you the most and skipping the others. Of course, you don't have to participate in every single suggestion, either. For example, not everyone has to go to a dating service, although I do recommend them if you possibly can. Dating services are, in effect, sophisticated agents. If you decide to forego them, make sure the rest of your agenting portion of the program, friends, professional acquaintances, is well oiled. And, not everyone has to begin a romance club; if not, there better be several other interest clubs to take up the slack. But everyone must take the self-inventory and keep a journal. The key is to participate fully in every section of the program. Whether you avoid bars and concentrate on private clubs, for another example, is up to you.

It takes time to change habits and beliefs, and it takes time to develop the social facility needed to express your best, or most appropriate, face. There are bound to be times when your efforts go unrewarded romantically. You'll become terribly frustrated and want to stop, wondering how such a seemingly simple exercise relates to your pursuit of romance. But don't give up. Work through these periods by concentrating on the thought that the program is actually a series of individual steps. Everything adds to the next step, even the moments of depression and so-called failure. For the program to work properly for you, it can't be done helter-skelter or whenever you feel in the mood. Its effects are cumulative.

Remember that we are trying to change an entire way of being and thinking. That process doesn't happen overnight. What doesn't feel comfortable today, may, by repetition, become second nature by a week from Sunday. Just as race car drivers don't speed around the Indianapolis track at two hundred miles per hour the day they learn to drive, neither should you feel that the program isn't working if you don't meet your life's mate immediately. Keep your standards and goals reasonable at first. Too many people try to go beyond what is reasonable. Setting their sights too high, they fail. Their failure creates discouragement, so they inevitably quit, blaming the program, but not their approach to it.

The mating game can be both fun and challenging. But in order to win at it, you must have a strategy you're willing to stick with.

Overcoming Shyness

While I never really conquered my shyness entirely, I have, you might say, made my peace with it; it's always there, and I'm aware of its presence, but now I can acknowledge it as almost a separate entity, apart from me. People who know me are surprised to hear stories of how my shyness shaped my personality, and they're astonished to learn I still consider myself shy. "You?" they say. "You're the last person I thought would be shy. You seem so congenial and confident."

It goes without saying that shyness can inhibit all social interaction, not the least of which is mate hunting. No one has to be completely free of shyness, indeed, no one is, but to find a mate, reducing the amount of social inhibition you feel will allow you to meet more people, and thus increase the number of choices you have. And that, after all, is the purpose of this book.

In the course of this chapter, I will be giving you some suggestions to help overcome the social inhibition you feel. Just as exercise reduces fat, conscientiously practicing these techniques will diminish the degree to which shyness governs your actions—or lack of them.

UNDERSTANDING SHYNESS

First, some insight into the nature of shyness; sometimes simply being aware of its machinations and dynamics allows people to begin to overcome it.

Shyness is a label applied to a profound group of afflictions, ranging from occasional mild awkwardness and embarrassment to social paralysis and agoraphobia. Typical social shyness, which affects almost everyone at least occasionally, can cause trepidation and uncertainty, particularly in new situations. Even people who are normally very aggressive tend to become meek and timid under special circumstances, such as when meeting others held in high esteem or when having to perform under pressure.

Social Paralysis and Phobias

Social paralysis or phobia, while less common, revolves around the fear of being judged; the opinion of others becomes so all-important, so consuming, that the social phobic feels he or she is being constantly judged, especially when in the presence of strangers. Consequently, alone or in familiar situations, everything is generally fine. Much like the child who fears the tyranny of adults and their authority, social phobics feel scrutinized and judged by others and they perceive the judgment to be negative, a reflection of their own low self-esteem.

The most severe form of shyness is, of course, the most rare: agoraphobia. Agoraphobics fear being in unfamiliar places, but the fear is so intense that they are often unable even to leave their homes, perhaps for years, without experiencing fainting, paralysis, dizziness, hyper-ventilation or other symptoms associated with panic attacks. Where the social phobic wants to disappear into the woodwork, the agoraphobic has to flee immediately or face the psychosymptomatic consequences.

I assume that few readers suffer from agoraphobia, and only a relative few from extreme social phobia. I also assume that most readers suffer from occasional bouts of social anxiety and uncertainty.

How Shyness Develops

Shyness begins in childhood. All children tend to be shy for the first two or three years of their lives. You can see them clutching at the legs of their mothers and fathers, peeking out carefully to see if the stranger giving them attention is safe. How the parent responds to the child's social fear will, in large part, determine how the grown child responds to social situations. If a parent is fearful for their child (especially these days, when newspapers are full of stories about child molestation and kidnaping) and unintentionally passes along that phobia, the child will learn to be afraid. The reinforced shyness then develops into an abnormal fear of unfamiliar people, places and situations, and eventually, it generalizes into a constant, gnawing anxiety which makes it impossible for the sufferer to function properly in the world.

Shyness may also develop in children who suffer an early loss of one or both parents. As a method of avoiding too much closeness or intimacy for fear of losing another loved one, they withdraw into themselves, hoping to erect an impenetrable shield as insulation from hurt. At the same time, the child with one remaining parent may cling pathetically to that parent, terrified of some unknown catastrophe occurring and making him an orphan. Likewise, the remaining parent may overprotect the child, feeling that the emotional attachment is essential support. Both situations encourage and intensify shyness.

Children with physical disabilities or severe childhood illnesses often develop into shy or fearful adults because they have been taught to be hyperafraid of hurting themselves or catching additional diseases. To these children, all strangers are viewed as threatening.

Chronic shyness in adults may also stem from other causes: frequent relocation of the family, which continually thrusts the child into unfamiliar situations and doesn't allow time for the child to establish close relationships with others of the same age; and very critical, demanding and perfectionist parents, whose children feel that they can never live up to the parents' expectations.

As children grow into adults, the manifestations of shyness evolve into more complex and subtle expressions. From clinging onto a parent's leg and begging not to be left alone at a school party, the older child may concoct an imaginary playmate with whom safety can be easily found. A few years later, the adolescent's imagination may construct elaborate fantasies as a method by which he or she regains some control over the world. And finally, the evolution is completed by adults who may develop grandiose styles in order to compensate for their underlying shyness and social inhibition. Amateur psychologists have, since World War II, referred to such personalities as overcompensating for an inferiority complex. The truth is closer to someone attempting to speak with headphones on while music is blasting: he can't hear his own words, so he yells unnecessarily at others who can.

To function as normally as possible, these people confine their experiences in order to avoid dealing with the full extent of their inhibitions. They may withdraw into their specific area of expertise, whether it be academia, auto mechanics, art, or whatever. In their own little universes, they are able to function entirely without anxiety, or minimal anxiety. It is only when forced to make contact outside of these spheres that their symptoms become apparent.

Adolescence. Certainly, many shy people lived in the same homes throughout their youths and had wonderful parents who encouraged independence. So what made them the way they are? Genes? The luck of the draw? A scary movie? While many factors are possible, including genetics, for some people the natural stresses of adolescence are traumatic enough to induce permanent emotional disability.

Almost all adolescents feel awkward; it comes with the territory. So many changes are occurring, physically, psychologically, socially, that the adolescent must constantly work to integrate them all. A teenager is painfully aware of and sensitive to criticism, peer pressure, and performance. Everything is experienced in a BIG WAY; everything that goes wrong is a catastrophe, while everything that goes right is "the best ever." Middle ground does not exist and neither does perspective. Look at the words teenagers use to describe impressions: devastated, crushed, blasted, blown away, annihilated. Mildly disappointing events are blown up bigger than life.

Adolescent experiences can leave scars that last for years, or a lifetime. So in later years, the young adult unwilling to admit immaturity must remember the event with equally overwhelming emotions in order to justify the experience of those feelings. Often then, what remains in adulthood is a larger-than-life reality, which doesn't respond to reason or facts, one which comforts the sufferer with a belief system intended to validate the sufferer's lack of self-esteem.

Tenacious Early Beliefs. As shy as I was in grammar school, I felt like a Vaudeville comedian compared to David, a boy who suffered from the most debilitating form of shyness, short of agoraphobia, I've ever seen. So painful was it for him even to speak, that he sat in class after class after class, year after year after year, without ever making the most minimal peep. Although an "A" student, and reasonably good looking, he endured in silent agony, his eyes always aimed at the ground or at his desk. It was obvious to everyone how painful school was for him. The school bullies, always anxious to pick on the most helpless students, actually ignored David, who was too pitiful even for them. He didn't have a single friend.

He never knew it, but David provided my most vivid memory of high school. It was in a Spanish class we had together. As in all classes, students were regularly called on, whether or not they raised their hands. By some tacit agreement between teachers, David was always spared the embarrassment of having to answer aloud (he probably always knew the answer). No one had ever heard his voice other than signifying "here," in a whisper, during roll calls. On this particular day, our Spanish teacher asked someone to answer an unusually difficult question; as I recall, it had something to do with the subjunctive. Since no one raised a hand to respond, she began to look around the room to find someone to answer. At that moment, David raised his hand. The normally raucous room immediately fell silent, all eyes focused on him. Even the teacher had a difficult time concealing her surprise. I speak for the majority, I'm sure, when I say that I found myself praying he wouldn't stammer. He didn't and answered the question correctly.

After another stunned silent moment, all of us broke into spontaneous, affectionate applause. For the just the briefest instant, David raised his head toward us and allowed a hint of a smile. I will never forget it.

While I had always wondered what caused him to be so horribly shy (I wonder to this day what became of him), it never occurred to me to ask until I was doing research for my doctoral thesis. I contacted a guidance counselor at my high school, who told me that the root cause of David's shyness was quite simply, but horribly, the belief that he had caused his mother's death. She had been stricken by cancer when he was three years old. As if that wouldn't have been traumatic enough, his father, never the sanest man to begin with, was driven almost over the edge by grief. Venting his rage one night, he told David, in the form of a bedtime story, that David had given the cancer to his mother; he made up a complex fantasy which, at David's tender age, seemed plausible enough. That belief began to infect every part of David's psyche, so that by the time, one year later, when he went to live with his aunt and uncle (his father was deemed not worthy to be a parent), he had withdrawn from the world—which he expected at any moment might punish him.

Even when, in young adulthood, his bright mind could evaluate the truth of his father's manic raving, the damage was too severe; it was more comforting, I suppose, to stay in his solitary prison.

Other children, responding to far less traumatic circumstances, respond similarly, if not as dramatically. Our assumptions, based either on fantasy or childish reality, can severely limit our adult actions. As small a thing as being criticized by for expressing a "stupid" opinion can inhibit a child, and later the adolescent and the adult, from again venturing an opinion in front of others.

Fears of Inadequacy and Rejection. Such early experiences of humiliation or embarrassment can have profound effects in later years, when the adult, seeking at all costs to avoid similar feelings, unconsciously invents situations in which slights, real or fantasized, occur. Imagining that potential rejection,the adult takes action based on the fearful possibility. In an unending cycle of projection and self-rejection, this person invents the worst fears out of, ironically, the fear of it coming to pass.

At their core, shy people dread being evaluated; they anticipate that their performance will not be adequate. Among children, test taking is one common form of anxiety associated with shyness. Adults fear that no one will like them, that they are unworthy of attention and affection, that they have nothing to offer. And if, by chance, they are given an opportunity to express themselves, they fear that they will be found out, exposed as shams.

Of course, such anxieties, whether they're as simple as test taking or as insidious as self-deprecation, become self-fulfilling. The anticipatory anxiety interferes with normal functioning, obscuring all abilities and positive traits. What remains after the fear of failure is only the failure itself, a failed grade or a failed attempt at relationships. "I can't succeed" becomes "I didn't succeed" begets "I can't succeed." "You couldn't like me, could you?" becomes "I knew it—you didn't like me" begets "I know you won't like me, but . . .." The worst-case scenario raises the shy person's fears and inhibitions, increasing the likelihood of that exact scenario occurring.

Reactions to Rejecton. Shy people seek to prevent further psychic damage by refusing to try for the fear of failure, the fear of fear. They call upon a core of memories in which their efforts weren't rewarded or appreciated, and they remember the laughter, real or imagined, of their detractors. Of course, they never intended to succeed, sabotaging their conscious intentions with the subconscious fear of humiliation, embarrassment or rejection. "I'd rather not try," they reason, "than get hurt." Again, the fear of fear.

The shy person's grossly exaggerated fears include the belief that an inept performance in a social situation will strike a fatal blow to their aspirations. "I will be absolutely ruined if I'm rejected," is the thought. Placing that expectation on the situation, making it life or death, creates a burden that is impossible to carry. Any attempt to shoulder that burden ensures certain failure.

The fundamental difference between shy people and more outgoing people seems to be encapsulated in their definitions of rejection. Outgoing people, comfortable in most social situations and unafraid to try to meet new people, define rejection much more narrowly than do shy people, who apply the term anytime someone doesn't jump into bed with them after saying "hello."

Logically, of course, there's no reason to feel rejected when a person you don't even know refuses to dance with you in a bar or at a party. There could be a pebble in her shoe, he could be nauseous from too many drinks, she could be with an incredibly insane boyfriend who carries a gun in his pocket, he could be allergic to the polyester blend in your dress, she could have two left feet and fear you won't like the way she dances, he could be gay, her hemorrhoids could have suddenly flared up, his bladder might be full, and so forth. Yet some of the most intelligent and successful people, engineers, doctors, lawyers, teachers and business people, feel that when they don't get what they want the moment they want it, they're being rejected. And they use that experience to justify not asking anyone else. This simple "no," attributable to who-knows-what, is seen as a mortal wound to the ego; the word itself becomes synonymous with abandonment.

On the other hand, people who are more outgoing and less shy view a "no" for exactly what it is, without feeling that their self-image has been stomped into the ground. Rejection, they recognize, is when someone whom they know and respect tells them, "Get away from me, you filthy pig, you and everything you represent disgust me," or, "If I ever see you again, you squamulose maggot, I'll call the police." Anything less than such unambiguous personality assessments is perceived as a simple stumbling block, not a brick wall.

If I were to cook you a dinner, and you refused to eat it, you wouldn't be rejecting me, would you? Of course not. You would be rejecting my food. The same is true with my ideas, my offers, my car, my taste in music, my opinions, my invitations.

ALTERING YOUR MIND-SET

Achieving a mind-set that will free you from the fear of rejection is the object of the progressive program I'm about to give you. In parentheses following each step is the recorded progress, as it related to that step, of one of my patients, who used this process to overcome her shyness and help her to meet others.

Step One: *List Your Fears*

Make a list of all the fears which keep you from making contact with other people. (Sara, a painfully shy twenty-six-year-old woman, was terrified that people would think she was too pushy, and maybe stupid, if she approached them; she talked only to people who spoke first to her, and not many did that, which she took as substantiation of her fears.)

Step Two: *Question Your Fears*

After having put aside the list for at least an hour, to gain some objectivity, study it carefully and question vigorously the validity of each reason. When was the last time whatever you feared actually occurred? (Sara couldn't remember any incidents in the recent past when anyone reacted negatively to her approaching them; she hadn't actually done so in many years.)

Step Three: *Compare Your Fears With Real Outcomes*

Ask yourself, what was the actual outcome of the horrendous event that makes you fear it so? (Sara recalled that, when she was in the fourth grade one of her classmates had apparently ignored her. Although she found out later that the girl was hard of hearing, that fact didn't change Sara's feelings because her mind-set was already established.)

Step Four: *Pinpoint Exaggerations*

Looking back over the list, decide honestly how many of the items have been exaggerated in order to substantiate your fear. (Sara realized that anytime anything embarrassing had happened to her, she was unable to view it as a passing incident and instead personalized the issue. In junior high school, for example, she had dropped some blood on her dress during a science project on hematology, and when some other students in the class began laughing at her, she believed they were laughing at her stupidity, and she ran crying out of the room. Even when her girlfriend tried to catch up to help her wash out her dress, Sara would not be consoled, feeling that no one liked her. Such events had long since been forgotten by her conscious mind, but their residual feelings remained. She later conveniently forgot that her friend had tried to help her.)

Set Five: *Ask yourself, "Am I Catastrophizing?"*

Ask yourself, "Am I 'catastrophizing'?" Are you constructing worst-case scenarios so terrible that no one would ever be able to act in the face of such catastrophe? (Each time she felt the urge to take the initiative and meet new people, Sara could see, in her mind's eye, other people laughing at her, as though they could see right through her and read her insecure thoughts. Those fearful thoughts always kept her from actually doing it, and eventually she gave up even the thought of trying.)

Step Six: *Put a Time-frame Around Your Fears*

Ask yourself, how many of your fears are based on assumptions, as opposed to current reality? Do you fear something that happened twelve years ago, not twelve days ago? (Obviously yes, in Sara's case.)

Step Seven: *Was It You Alone to Blame?*

Ask yourself, how many of your reasons can be attributed to factors other than something being wrong with you personally? Was it you or the circumstances that inspired the fear? (When she examined the facts objectively, Sara could see that her reluctance to talk to other people gave her an air of superiority, of conceit, and that the reason other people tended to avoid her was because of those attitudes they believed she exuded. Her feelings of embarrassment and self-ridicule were so great that she had forgotten all of the circumstances and incidents that caused her to make the decisions she had. Once she had these realizations, Sara was freer to explore contact with others, and much to her amazement, they responded.)

Having begun to challenge the assumptions on which your fear of social contact is based, and having questioned whether you are exaggerating your fears or making wild assumptions in order to justify your behavior, you are ready to reconnect your feelings to reality and current experience.

A BRIEF COURSE IN OVERCOMING SHYNESS

Using this process as a base, I am now going to give you an abbreviated course on overcoming shyness. It is certainly not a panacea and will not immediately give you the courage to stand on the corner flagging down attractive people, but if followed diligently, it can take you a long way into the social arena. If possible, work with a partner or two. This should not be a trial by ordeal, and taking along a supportive person (from your Romance Club, perhaps) can make the experience fun. The entire mini-program extends over a six-week period, and is progressive; step two is easier because of step one, step three is easier because of step two, and so on. By the time you reach the last step, you will be doing things you thought you might never be able to muster the courage to do.

Now, get out your journal and record your experiences, keeping a record of your thoughts, feelings, impressions, and realizations so that you remember them. Both the act of recording them and looking back over them will ultimately be two significant steps in helping you to overcome shyness.

Week One: *Say Hello to five people a day*.

The purpose of this exercise is to become comfortable merely saying "hello" to people. They must be five people you have never seen before, male or female, and you need not have romantic intentions in mind. In fact, you don't even need to carry on further conversation.

Just as if you were stretching before a jog, this exercise is meant to warm you up. While it isn't the most strenuous task in the world, most people have a fairly difficult time saying a simple hello. Shy people, particularly, find that the word gets stuck their throat, their mouth drying up like a roll of cotton. Their fear? Who knows? According to the information I've gathered over the years, no one has ever been killed for saying hello to someone in an elevator or supermarket. Quite the contrary; usually the person receiving the hello likes it and smiles back. Don't you?

A small thing, you may think, but after seven full days you will have said hello to thirty-five people. And that's not small.

Week Two: *To another five people a day, add a compliment of some sort—on their shoes, their smile, their work,
their anything.*

They do not have to be the previous week's hello
people; it may be impossible to find the same guy walking
past you on the street. If possible though, and depending
on your inclination, you may indeed want to compliment
the same people (particularly if you have romantic designs).

Compliments are excellent icebreakers. Very few
people do not like to hear that they look nice or have
done something well. Compliments serve to make an ally
out of the person complimented, and they can prove to be
preludes to further conversation.

At the end of this second week, you will have said
hello to thirty-five people and complimented thirty-five
people.

One shy young man I helped to find a mate some
years ago realized about 11 PM one night that he hadn't
yet filled his quota for the day. So he dressed quickly and
ran down to his neighborhood 7-Eleven store, where he
say hello to and complimented the first three people who
came in. At first he was embarrassed, but then it became
a challenge to him, almost like a game. The third person,
a young woman, turned out to be especially friendly, and
the two of them retired for the night to a diner, where
they talked until 2 AM. (No, they didn't get married.)

Week Three: *Have an actual conversation with five
people a day.*

Of course, I'm not expecting you to achieve new
heights of witty repartee, necessarily, but I do want you to

at least integrate the hello with a compliment and a couple extra words. Example:

"Hi."
"Hello."
"Nice day, isn't it?"
"Yes, it is."
"I like your sweater."
"Thanks."
"Have a nice day."
"You too."

And that's all. Obviously, anything beyond that is icing. In fact, if you feel up to it, review the previous chapters on communication and go for it; try any of the techniques.

For those of you who felt okay about weeks one and two but are terrified now, your first instinct may be to think that you don't come across five people a day with whom conversation is possible. How about the supermarket checker, the dry cleaner, the car wash attendant, a policeman, the UPS man, a passenger on the bus, the driver of the next car in a traffic jam, a bank teller? Get out of the house; you're bound to run into people everywhere.

After these three weeks, you will have made contact with at least one hundred people.

You will be a professional at saying hello. You will be a semipro at dishing out compliments. And you will be a novice at starting conversations.

Remember, do not become despondent if your conversations don't ascend to sublimity. Understand that there is another person at the other end of your mouth who also bears responsibility for the conversation's progress. Don't blame yourself for the other person's inability to contribute to the dialogue. If one gives flat, one-word responses, you may have found someone who is just as shy as you are.

Keep your expectations for these conversations low. Let them gather their own momentum, and if they don't, that's all right, too; eventually they will. Have patience. As Lao-Tsu, the ancient Chinese philosopher, said, "The journey of a thousand miles begins with a single step."

Week Four: *Your assignment this week is to visit five bars or night clubs, discos, cocktail lounges, or other informal social gathering places.*

These places, as you should remember from chapters six and seven, are wonderful for practicing technique because you are unlikely ever to see again the people on whom you'll be practicing. What's more, these places are filled with people who want to meet others, so they're open for conversation, if nothing more.

While their practiced looks of insouciance convey don't-touch-me vibes, they are mostly willing to make contact; they're trying to protect themselves from being rejected or hurt, just like you. If they appear as though they are untouchable, and no one tries to make contact, then they have a ready excuse to justify their solitude, to themselves. In honest conversations with many, the truth arises: somewhere along the line, probably from the posed models in advertisements, they got the impression that nonchalance was sexy.

If, however, nightclubs and cocktail lounges scare you too much, try out department stores or special interest clubs, anywhere there are people. The advantage to night spots is their supply of readily available and willing singles. But in any event, you don't have to feel the pressure of meeting them this week. Your assignment is strictly familiarization.

Accordingly, make certain that you feel comfortable in whichever locale you choose. First, get to know the parking lot. I realize that may sound somewhat silly to you, but believe me, it really helps. Think of it as building a foundation. Park your car and retrieve it a few times before entering the place.

Then locate the bathrooms.

In fact, you may want to park your car, go inside and visit the bathroom, then exit and get in your car to leave several times before making your first move. Besides getting you acquainted with the physical layout, such an exercise can hasten your retreat to a safe and familiar spot should it be necessary, that is, should you lose confidence and begin to panic.

In the event your stomach begins turning over, your hands drip sweat and your lip quivers, do not leave. Simply collect yourself by visiting your car or the now-recognizable bathroom. You are not there to perform, you are there to meet people, people, in many cases, as shy as you are. There are no judges, no audience and no scores coming in. They are just folks. A shy patient of mine told me that when he considered people "folks," and conversations "chats," he found it much easier to approach them and begin conversations.

Visit several bars or lounges to find the five which feel most comfortable. If you have to, visit ten or twenty or one hundred to find the five you can handle. Just observe the patrons there, what they do, what they say, how they act. The only dialogues you need to strike up are with the bartenders and waiters/waitresses. The same simple conversations you tried with others last week are your aim here. These, however, should be easier. Bartenders and waiters are there to serve you and want both your business and your tip; and besides, they generally like people.

Week Five: *Having spoken in vague terms to the employees in week four, your job now is to talk with them about the establishment itself.*

Find out from them as much as you can about the place, its patrons, its owners, anything that may help you to maintain contact with them. If you'd like, you can tell them you're doing research for a bar guide. Hearing that, most people want to provide valuable assistance and will go to some extremes to find answers to questions they themselves do not know. This phenomenon has something to do with the instant credibility attributed to the media, much the way that, in retail stores, signs for products often say, "As seen on TV."

Once you feel comfortable talking with the employees, it is a great deal easier to make contact with the patrons. Often, in fact, the one leads naturally enough to the other.

Week six: *Have a conversation with at least five people in a bar, lounge, or any other places in which you decided you were comfortable.*

Now don't panic. Just make the same sort of conversation you did in week three. And you don't have to talk to five in one night. You may spread it out over three nights, or five, or even seven. Remember: You are there to talk with people, people who are, in many cases, as shy as you.

It's likely that the thought of striking up five conversations in a bar can send you into conniptions; believe me, I know. But if you have taken the six weeks step by step, week six is going to be a thousand percent simpler than it now seems. I promise.

By the time you reach this point in the process, you will have spoken to so many people, making the contact you never thought possible. Simple conversation in a bar will not be an excruciating adventure. You will be essentially a different person. Just as a diver jumping off the hundred-foot cliffs at Acapulco begins at one foot, then moves to five feet high, then ten, twenty, thirty, and so on, you will have become comfortable wading into these social waters.

Once You Get There

When I was picking up take-out at a Chinese a restaurant in New York, I ran into a woman I'd admired from afar in high school. Still very attractive, she had had the reputation of being one of the most beautiful girls in the twelfth grade. The moment we recognized each other, I remembered vividly how strongly I had been attracted to her. So totally had she captured my imagination and inspired my adolescent sexual fantasies, it was not until a time well past college and graduate school that she was finally displaced as the standard by which I measured feminine beauty. Now, a decade or so later, what surprised me most was that she actually remembered me.

A STARTLING REVELATION

Then came the most startling revelation. Over coffee, she confessed that she, too, had had a major crush on me.

I couldn't believe it, and, like the awkward teenager I had been the last time we saw each other, I became tongue-tied. Embarrassed and shocked, I told her I doubted her claim.

"No, really, I did," she said, no doubt aware that she had just flattered me beyond comprehension. "There was always something about you that I was attracted to. Something different."

Me? She was saying these things to me? If only she could have known—if only I could have told her—how many of my fantasies she had dominated, and for how many years. I told her, laughingly, that it must be obvious I would have sold my mother to the Cossacks for her.

"Then why didn't you ask me out?" she said.

The answer to that question, in a nutshell, is what this chapter is all about.

I gave her only a cursory response then: I had assumed she didn't like me because I never received an engraved invitation from her. But in the days and weeks following our meeting, I devoted much deeper thought to all the reasons for my failure to ask her out, not because my life was any less rich without her, but because I knew that whatever factors kept me from realizing my fantasies probably also prevented other people from doing the same.

While lack of confidence and fear of rejection certainly had contributed to my lack of action, they were reinforced by ignorance: not knowing how to make contact, how to flirt, how to make my intentions known, and which signs of interest to watch for.

Of course, in failing to convey her wishes clearly, she bore as much responsibility as I for our inability to connect.

If Only I Had Known

And that, in a nutshell, was the most important bit of wisdom to arise from this meeting: one person, taking the initiative, can bring together two people who otherwise would have wandered by each other, wondering. How many potential mates have we all passed up, simply because we were too ignorant to take action?

In your own life, how many times have you discovered that someone you had been interested in had also been interested in you, yet you both had done nothing? How many times have you found yourself wishing: If only I knew then what I know now?

Like anything else in life, learning to make contact with romantic intentions takes practice. In the previous chapter, we practiced, among other things, just saying hello to people. Now we're going to take it one step further.

THE ART OF SMALL TALK

Making small talk is an art which has been largely forgotten. People tend to discredit cocktail conversation, claiming it's shallow and phony. But it has its purpose. How else can you ever get to the heavy, meaningful dialogue? I doubt that you would think me very interesting, or sane, if I approached you on a park bench and asked whether Nietzsche's fundamental contribution to European culture was the namesake of a cartoon super hero. However, if we first chatted about, say, the weather, and moved the conversation logically from meteorology to science to philosophy, you might then understand my intended meaning.

Small talk must come as a prelude. It is an invitation to contact, just as openness is an invitation to intimacy.

To decide what topic to use as the conversation's ice-breaker, refer to the location of the encounter. In the waiting room of a doctor's office, for example, the topic may be the length of time spent waiting, or the (poor?) selection of magazines.

In the supermarket, again, just for practice, and not necessarily with romance as your goal, notice the kinds of goods the person in front of you is placing on the checkout counter. Use whatever is obvious, whatever is easiest for you. If there is, say, a can of cat food, use that as an icebreaker.

Ask what kind of cat this person has, and maybe how old the animal is. So much the better if you also have a cat. The idea is just to talk, to get the other person talking, to make contact. Some items are perhaps best left unmentioned. For instance, remarking on the softness of a particular toilet tissue is considered bad form, as would be your praise for the deodorant qualities of a certain brand of feminine hygiene spray.

If you are in the produce section, and the person you're interested in happens to be fondling the eggplants, ask him or her how to pick out a good eggplant, if there is such a thing. You can even ask how it's best prepared.

At a sporting event, if you see someone you like getting a hot dog, use the obvious, the event itself, as an opening gambit. "Boy, (the team) sure is playing lousy (or great) this evening. I haven't seen them play like this in years."

Use anything you can, anything at hand or obvious, to make contact. As long as the icebreaker leaves room for a response, and it isn't offensive, you have something on which to build. The icebreaker is only a foundation, nothing more.

For our purposes, any public locale is appropriate as a practice arena for icebreakers, and you need not necessarily be attracted to the person with whom you're practicing technique. The reason I'm mentioning such places as supermarkets and doctor's offices is because people don't usually think to make contact with others there; I want to show that contact can be made anywhere. In fact, if you're searching for someone whose primary interest is cooking, then a supermarket is indeed a place to frequent, particularly the gourmet sections. And all of these places are appropriate when searching for a play-mate; you never know when you'll get lucky. When trying to make contact in a hobby or interest club, you don't have to be as subtle, because primary contact, and common ground, has already been established; by the same token, other club members who decline to go along with your conversation are telling you implicitly that they're there for one reason only, and it's not you.

Flattery

It may be a cliche, but flattery will get you everywhere, or at least to a lot of places. Flattery disarms people, tending to make them more vulnerable.

Like small talk, there is an art to flattery as an ice-breaker. Eye contact must first be made, otherwise a comment, such as, "You have very beautiful eyes," or, "That's a great looking sweater," might be dismissed as a casual remark. Then, while holding the eye contact, smile. Not many people will misunderstand your intentions.

Body Language

Once the initial contact is made, the next thing to be aware of is body language. It is the first method, and one of the most reliable, of judging a person's initial interest in you. Body language is something we all speak, all the time and usually without either our consent or knowledge.

Words say one thing, but bodies may say something else entirely, and usually more honestly. Many times a person will profess an interest in getting to know you, while walking in the opposite direction. Well, how can you say you want to get to know me when you're not even willing to stand still? At best, such action indicates ambivalence; at worst, it's lying, pure and simple.

Our bodies register our receptiveness and willingness to receive input from other people and situations. Arms crossed across the chest, a tight or uptight frame, limbs scrunched closely together; together suggest an impenetrability, an unwillingness to make contact.

Do a quick check of your own body: clenched fists or teeth show anger, sweaty palms and a tight stomach mean nervousness or anxiety, a downturned mouth indicates unhappiness. Your body is a sophisticated instrument, responding to internal stimuli and reacting appropriately, giving signals to others without the conscious mind interfering in the process. It's a very rare person indeed who can be aware enough of his body's language to consciously change it for the purpose of hiding his true feelings.

The exceptions to that rule are actors, trained to speak with their bodies as well as their voices. In fact, to improve your skills in understanding body language, you can practice by watching television with the sound off. Try to guess the emotional tone, conflict and outcome of each scene through the actors' gestures and facial contortions.

After you've achieved some proficiency watching actors, study real people. Sit on a park bench or go to a party, anyplace where you can observe people interacting. If you're within earshot, try to tune out the conversation, just as you did with the television, and see how close you can come to understanding what's going on merely by watching how they cross and uncross their arms and legs, bend, lean over, scrunch up, stand, sit, and crane their necks. Then, to check yourself, listen if you can to their words. In the cases when you're interpretation was wrong, tune out the conversation again and recheck yourself. Practice, practice, practice.

Between men and women, there are specific hints to watch for which indicate precourtship behavior. If the person you are interested in begins to emulate your behavior or posture, changing positions subconsciously to mirror yours, you can be reasonably sure you are liked. Preening behavior, such as stroking the hair, means a desire to appear attractive. A slight tilt of the head to expose the neck indicates vulnerability; this gesture is a vestige of our animal heritage. Pelvic thrusts, moving in such a way as to extend the hips outward, are suggestive and show a willingness to make contact, as does fiddling with shirt buttons, which likewise symbolizes eroticism. Occasionally, one person will flick a piece of lint or dirt off the shoulder of the other. Like any physical contact, this is a positive signal to proceed, whether or not the one doing the flicking knows it consciously.

Being on the receiving end of negative body language takes an even more studious approach in order to gauge disinterest correctly. If the person turns away while answering your icebreaking question, then you're probably not going to be friends this time around. If the person refuses to make eye contact with you, then the same conclusion may be reached. Sure, we've all seen movies or television shows in which a man tries to pick up a woman who's plainly not interested in him, yet his persistence eventually pays off and they jump into the sack together. Well, forget it, the movies are not real life. Should you be convinced that the object of your intentions has turned purposely away from you, both bodily and visually, then move on yourself. Don't force the issue. And don't waste time.

There are, of course, other reasons why someone may not appear to be interested in you: he or she is having a particularly bad day or something else was pressing at that moment are two common ones.

But the most obvious may be personal hygiene.

Let me tell you a story which illustrates well enough the need for personal hygiene. When I was in college, all the hep people were English majors, interested in literature and poetry. And all the best-looking girls, it seemed to me, were included in that group. Since I hadn't done spectacularly well on the romantic scene, I figured that if I could get close to some of those hep cats, I could score. So I enrolled in an American literature class given by a poet of some renown. I knew there were bound to be several girls there who fit the description.

Sure enough, on the first day the class met, I spotted her. She was gorgeous, blond hair spilling over her black turtleneck, green eyes brooding with the intensity of beat poetry.

Too nervous to approach her immediately, I watched her for a couple weeks and formulated a plan. Finally, I made my move, arriving at class early enough to sit in the seat next to her. With a copy of Allen Ginsberg's "Howl" placed cunningly and conspicuously on top of my books, I anxiously said hello; she was the most beautiful female I had ever been close to. She looked at me, her eyes washing over me hypnotically. She could have, at that moment, demanded I stick a hot knife through my eye and I would have considered it.

But when she said hello back to me, I got a lot more than I'd anticipated. To put it frankly, her breath smelled like she'd been gargling with sewage. Wow. My eyes began to burn, my anxiety turned to nausea, and my interest, well, shriveled.

Still, wanting both to give her the benefit of the doubt and to see my plan through to the end, particularly since she had responded as I had only imagined and was still the most beautiful girl ever to talk to me, I sat next to her at the following class. Unfortunately, the gnats still swarmed around her mouth, and I had to find another seat.

Wherever she is now, I hope she corrected the problem; either that, or married a man with no nose. So check your personal hygiene. Which is, anyway, only common sense. Enough said on that topic.

Back to body language. On the positive side, if the person maintains a body position, facing you, it's worth it to continue exploring the possibilities. At worst, a body squared to you with the head turned indicates ambivalence; at best, it's a kind of shyness.

If eye contact is made as your icebreaker is answered, then you know you've got an excellent chance, particularly if the gaze is held. Further, if you see eyes exploring your face, especially the lips, you've just observed a come-on sign.

The danger in relying too heavily on body language is that we will project our own personalities onto the other person. If you are the eternal optimist, you may refuse to believe that a complete pirouette and obstinately clenched fist mean "get lost." The dedicated pessimist may fail to see that seventeen pelvic thrusts, an unbuttoned shirt and outstretched arms are an invitation. So be careful, and as objective as possible.

Shifting the Conversation

Now, assuming you've made contact and the body language says "let's see what you've got" and the eye contact is powerful, perhaps the eyes are even exploring your face, the next thing is to change the conversation.

The point of changing the conversation is to see, without wasting a great deal of either your time or the other person's, whether there is interest in pursuing some sort of relationship, or at least interest enough to investigate pursuing some sort of relationship. While many people will respond to an opening gambit and perhaps seem interested, through body language and eye contact, even when they aren't, very rarely will they accommodate a shift in conversation without some genuine interest as a motivator. Although continuing a conversation is not a foolproof method of judging romantic intentions, it does guarantee enough interest to talk further.

For your part, be subtle. Suppose you've begun your conversation in the produce section with an inquiry about eggplants, and the other person has responded by helping you pick out a tasty one. So move from the specific, the eggplant itself, to the more general. Ask, for example, if they like to cook. In other words, see if you can continue the conversation beyond the initial question.

What you are looking for is any kind of dialogue that goes beyond the concrete eggplant question. If the person follows your lead, answering your question, then you have just received an important piece of information. You may then move the conversation in any direction you choose, including, expressing an interest in sampling, first-hand, each others cooking abilities.

Let me give you another example. Suppose you are a man in a department store, shopping for a tie, and you see a woman you think you could be interested in. Your ice-breaker may be asking her, explaining that you're not very good at matching colors, whether this particular tie goes with that particular shirt. If she answers the question specifically and then moves on, the game is over. However, if she says no, then begins looking through the rack with you to find a tie that does match, you've made a connection. Not only has she given you advice, she's changing venue, which is, in itself, a positive sign. (Generally speaking, asking about eggplant in the shirt section of a department store is not a good icebreaker.)

Since she may, after all, be exceedingly friendly but happily married to the heavyweight champion of the world and curious to see if men still find her attractive, or unhappily married to the karate champ of the world, it's important to ask yourself, Why is she in the men's department? So inquire, discreetly, as to the purpose of her presence there: "Looking for a birthday gift for your husband?"

On the other hand, she may (ladies, please change the genders and milieus accordingly) be doing as one of my patients did when single: cruise the lingerie departments of fine department stores, pretending to seek assistance in buying a gift for his mother. He always emphasized, right off the bat, that the gift was for his mother, because he naturally didn't want to convey the message that he was attached in any way.

By the same token, pay attention yourself to any subtle references made to boyfriends, girlfriends, husbands and wives, in any locale and any conversation. These usually mean that the person in question is not interested in pursuing a relationship. Likewise, in the supermarket, a shopping cart filled to the brim with groceries probably means that the shopper is buying for more than one person, so inquire discreetly for whom the bell peppers toll.

Wherever you are, make certain your icebreaker is neither too corny nor too aggressive; then check body language, looking especially for face-to-face and squared shoulder contact; and then watch for eye contact, noting any probing, direct stares as a positive sign and any distant and cold gazes as probable I'm-not-interesteds. Keep the conversation focused until you feel reasonably certain that the other person is expressing interest, and then change topics.

If the other person introduces new subject matter into the conversation, you can, literally and figuratively, feel free to push your shopping cart alongside.

On the other hand, make your assumptions carefully, because some shy people who are otherwise interested may answer any questions but turn away quickly for fear of being caught looking at you, even though the conversation was initiated by you. (See Chapter Seven on Shyness) The question you always have to answer is, Is it worth pursuing? Apparent disinterest or ambivalence may not be what it seems. Eventually, with practice, you'll be able to tell the difference between them. And you won't have to run down a checklist taped to your wrist to make sure you're doing it correctly; the process will, with practice, become like second nature.

FLIRTING

In essence, I suppose, what I am trying to teach you to do successfully is to flirt. Flirting has become something of a lost art over the last decade, falling into disregard as sexual expectations and mores allowed, indeed invited, the most blatant kind of overtures and innuendoes. Moreover, flirting's reputation has recently been hurt by people who are always on the make, pushing themselves obnoxiously and incessantly on an unending stream of sexual targets.

Real flirting is much more subtle. Like successful mating, it's an attitude, a consciousness, a way of being. Flirting means adopting a romantic, in the broadest sense, way of relating to the world; inviting it into your boudoir, so to speak.

When a person skilled in flirting turns it on, you may not even know where it comes from or what's happening to you; it exudes, rather than exhibits. It's more demure, a stance, rather than a position; an invitation, not a demand; a statement of availability, not a hijacking.

The Clothes You Wear

To study flirting, you need to look not just at flirtatious behavior, but at the whole package, including clothing and stance. What one wears and how one wears it are vitally important. Certain clothing, like painted camouflage (á la Rambo) designs, conveys standoffishness; while other garments, such as cashmere, imply accessibility.

If I were a stiff, uptight man wearing a three-piece suit, standing stiffly and uptightly near the bar with a kind of distant gaze in my eye, the attitude I'd be giving off is that I'm still working, still mentally at the office, so don't bother me; I'd not likely be mistaken for exuding flirtatious vibes.

This isn't to say, necessarily, that three-piece suits are, in and of themselves, inappropriate for flirting; one can certainly flirt in a three-piece suit. I'm only using the three-piece as a representative example. There are certainly some venues where three-piece suits are completely appropriate. Just as some dogs seem scarier, more menacing, than other breeds, some kinds of clothing are more foreboding than others. They emit what can be construed as cautionary messages.

Softer fabrics, on the other hand, seem more sensual, more inviting. They seem to say, "touch me," which is, after all, the point of flirting, if not yet physically, at least mentally or emotionally.

No matter what you wear, from a three-piece suit to a camouflage jumpsuit, you can express a certain relaxed style through body posture. Change it from authoritarian to relaxed: leg bent, not stiff; shoulders off-center, not squared. Project a countenance of approachability.

Think, again, of Cary Grant, who could, somehow, make the three-piece suit or tuxedo look seductive. Cary looked women in the eye with an unmistakable sexuality that was inviting. Even though he stood well over six feet tall, he had a way of comporting himself that wasn't foreboding. It was his elegant attitude. In varying degrees, the same may be said of Fred Astaire, Charles Boyer, Myrna Loy, Grace Kelly and Ingrid Bergman, all of whom had an irresistible charm, presence and charisma.

While most of us, of either sex, can't duplicate the *je ne sais quoi* of these people, we can look and dress the part, as well as develop a personal style. There are a few important tips I can and will pass along your way, but unfortunately, there are no magic potions to make you stylish. The key, as with many aspects of life, is simply to like yourself and other people. Because without that feeling, you may transmit the kitschy sort of come-on vibes satirized by Steve Martin and Dan Ackroyd on "Saturday Night Live," when they played those "wild and crazy Czechoslovakian guys" in search of "big American breasts." That kind of caricatured behavior tries to overcompensate for a lack of self appreciation. "Hey, don't you love me?" people like that seem to be saying. They may have all the right stuff, like jewelry, fast cars and designer drugs, but they don't have the right stuff: self-respect and a genuine caring for others.

Genuineness

The attitude you'd ideally like to cultivate, even if you're not looking for a permanent mate, is one of genuineness. You can, if you wish, go out there and get laid every night but still feel and express a caring for the object of your temporary affections. I know people who have many one-night stands, but care for every one of their partners for however long the encounter lasts.

Skeptical? How about the unnaturally quick intimacy that develops on an airplane between passengers who, having never seen each other before, will reveal things about themselves over the course of a five-hour flight they may have never told anyone else; yet when they see each other at the baggage claim, the intimacy has already dissipated. The same is true with, if you remember, summer camp romances.

Situations such as those inspire a form of bonding because each party is open, without pretenses to shield their vulnerability. A common experience draws them together, and in that context a meaningful exchange, engendered by vulnerability, the invitation to connect is established.

Too many people are just on the prowl, so when they want to become intimate, they just don't know how; they've never practiced it. Humanity is the quality people respond to most in others. When even unattractive people express it, they become more appealing. No one has to look like Robert Redford or Linda Evans to be attractive. Conversely, if Redford and Evans weren't the caring people they are purported to be, they wouldn't be as appealing looking.

Thinking about this topic always reminds me of a boy I went to high school with. At his best, Howard was average looking. Yet he consistently dated the most beautiful girls, including the one I had the crush on and later ran into in the Chinese restaurant. You didn't have to be Einstein or Freud to figure out that what these girls liked about him and were attracted to was his obvious kindness, his vulnerability and caring.

Developing That Certain Style

The question is, how do we develop that certain style if it doesn't seem to come naturally? First, check and recheck your personal inventory sheet. Pay particular attention to the values you have elevated in both yourself and others. Do they emphasize warmth and sincerity, or superficialities? Do these characteristics seem to jibe with what you feel to be your day-to-day attitudes? Do you genuinely like the opposite sex, like them as people? When you leave the house to find members of the opposite sex, do you view it as an adventure whose purpose is to meet people, or simply an opportunity to score? Will it be a competitive, combative outing, as if stalking prey, or an invitation to get to know you?

Second, bearing the answers to all these questions in mind, imagine yourself with either an infant, a puppy or a kitten, whichever gives you personally the most pleasure. When thinking about one or all of these little creatures, most people feel a softening, a gentleness, enveloping them. Then imagine approaching one of them. What is the attitude you project? It's likely that you feel warm and exhibit warmth; there's a smile on your face, indicative of the openness you feel; it's almost palpable. Because you don't feel the need to protect yourself, you radiate a vulnerability, the quality which makes you attractive to the little one, and you express softness and caring.

Become aware of this feeling in a way that allows you to call upon it when you wish. Exuding it, not necessarily in a wimpy, mushy, coochy-coo manner, acts both to soften your approach to people and to enable them to appreciate you. Essentially, you will be attracted through appreciating each other's vulnerability. This is, by the way, a method actors use to emote whatever is appropriate to the scene they're playing. They call upon a memory of an experience designed to arouse the feeling called for by the part, knowing that as their emotions lead, their physical characteristics follow.

Add to that a softer body posture and more accessible clothing, then let the first words out of your mouth express flattery or positive acknowledgement or appreciation of the person with whom you are flirting, and you will find the experience more rewarding, that is, the rewards will increase.

You Don't Have to Appear Seductive

It is not necessary to appear obviously seductive in order to flirt successfully. In fact, such an approach has become fairly dated, and seems caricatured, at best, except in certain sadomasochist bars. For men who appreciate women and women who appreciate men, the combative, aggressive style seems contrived and is, anyway, often a turn-off; the person doing it seems to be pretending to be on the make.

By changing the encounter from adversarial, coming on as if trying to find a partner to shoot craps with, to mutually supportive, you allow yourself to be known and others to know you. And that is your goal, whether you're searching for a permanent mate or a playmate.

The same sort of intimacy and genuineness that develops on airplanes and in summer camp can in occur in bars and clubs, and on park benches and street corners, wherever you and another person make contact. It depends, of course, on your attitude.

The Hospitable Personality

When inviting guests into your home, you offer them your hospitality, and certainly you prefer to invite in people whom you believe you have a reasonable chance of liking or caring about. Well, you are, in a sense, inviting guests into your personality, making them welcome in your heart and mind. Doing it hospitably, you create situations which are filled with possibilities, whether your intentions are for the night or forever. Your life is your party, and whom you want to invite into it is up to you. You make the rules, you draw up the guest list, and you send out the invitations (remember that a pleasant invitation is more likely to elicit a positive R.S.V.P. than a nasty one). And just because your invitation is rejected doesn't mean that something is wrong with you; any number of explanations may be valid, including that the other person is a jerk.

I don't expect that the simple memory of being nine years old and seeing the movie *Old Yeller* will successfully arouse the softness and vulnerability you need each time you flirt. But I do expect that you will use similar experiences to practice your technique, in front of the mirror and/or with your Romance Club.

Facial Expressions

Practice a caring look. Practice a sympathetic look. Practice an interested look and an angry look and an enthusiastic look and every other look you can. Practice, practice, practice. While such an exercise may sound robotic and contrived, I promise you will be surprised by the results, particularly if you have the opportunity to use a video camera in the presence of others whom you trust to judge you objectively and without malice (your Romance Club).

One of my patients years ago was a wonderful, caring, committed woman. She had a chiseled face that looked hard and cold, with apparently uncaring green eyes, and if you didn't know her well you would have sworn she was someone to avoid. In fact, her facial characteristics did cause her problems.

As part of her job, she had to engage in periodic feedback sessions with her colleagues in which each had to honestly critique everyone else. During the first session she attended, she received consistently negative reports. Most said she was standoffish and distant. She came to me in tears. She wanted to know how she could be so misunderstood. I suggested that she practice, in front of a mirror, changing her countenance. She did so diligently, practicing making her facial expressions seem more accessible.

Six weeks later, she was judged the most accessible executive in her group, a position she retained throughout most of her two years at the company.

Learn what your own facial expressions look like. Examine whether they honestly portray your feelings inside. If not, change them. Are the corners of your mouth turned down, as if in anger? Have you unintentionally affected a distant, aloof attitude to mask your shyness? The answers to these questions may be surprising. For all your good intentions, the face you show to the world may not be the one you believe it is. People are often shocked to find out that they look like Jack the Ripper when they feel like Mary's little lamb.

Learn how to alter your expressions. See if your friends and/or club members can guess which emotion is written on your face. By just moving your head, practice sending messages, that is, conveying feelings, until the meaning they receive always connects with your intention. If possible, use a video camera, as it allows you to stand back and critique your performance without having to perform at the same time.

Then practice adding in words, making sure that their meaning, too, always connects with what your face says. Then add body posture, to be sure that it aligns with your face and words. Just as Archibald Leach practiced becoming someone called Cary Grant and so eventually became him, you must practice allowing your face to express the vulnerability you intend.

Practice and feedback, practice and feedback, practice and feedback.

I know that some people are reluctant to take part in this portion of the program, feeling it silly and unnecessary. But when I remind them that, as teenagers, they probably took part in a very similar process, mimicking in front of the mirror the stances and mannerisms of (choose the appropriate name or names) Elvis Presley, Frank Sinatra, Janis Joplin, John Lennon, Grace Kelly, Madonna, or Marlon Brando they laugh in acknowledgement. The difference is that, in youth, cool disaffection was often the goal; now, it's openness and vulnerability. And, in fact, I find that it is quite often those images, planted in youth, which this exercise must eliminate.

Firm eye contact and a genuinely inviting smile, reflecting a warmth from within, are what flirting is all about. Eye contact establishes the connection, while the smile disarms.

It is at this point, after all your practice and hard work, that the rewards begin. A smile will be returned, followed perhaps by a slight turning of the head to indicate intimacy, and you will be aware for the first time of every element, every seemingly unrelated thread, coming together into a beautiful tapestry.

"That which is expressed," said Aristotle, "is impressed." Smile.

Intimacy

In my practice as a psychologist, I have heard hundreds of patients complain about as many troubles and somatic ailments as the imagination can invent. Yet the one problem which seems to crop up consistently has to do with intimacy, either the inability to achieve it or the manic need to have it at any cost.

My purpose in showing you how to meet potential mates was not, in and of itself, an end. My purpose was to help you realize your goal, spoken or unspoken, of achieving intimacy with others. And I would be remiss if, after getting you to the point where you have the opportunity to choose from a selection of potential significant others, I signed off without even a word about intimacy. I want your relationships to work. Once you've found a mate, I want you to have the tools to keep your mate and to enjoy a satisfying relationship.

It's a well known fact that about half of all marriages in this country end in divorce, with the ratio in some parts of the country even higher. Some people attribute this to our unrealistically high expectations, which cause us to believe that the first sign of difficulty means the relationship isn't perfect. We expect that the relationship we've been searching for, the one we believe we've just found, will be a panacea for all our troubles, wiping away our unhappiness, transforming our lives into peaceful bliss. We want this other person to fulfill us, as if we cannot do it ourselves.

Some people, in fact, are on constant alert, quick to ordain each new relationship "The One" which will succeed, where all others have previously failed to make them complete human beings. But that type of neediness and desperation, having to be completed, as it were, by another, soon turns off the dominant partner, who usually turns and runs. Whether or not the one running away indeed fears intimacy or is just unable to cope with that neediness, the needy partner perceives his or her lost lover as manifesting strength, which in turn adds to the mystique and triggers further neediness.

Another phenomenon common in the high-expectations genre is the misbelief that mates can fulfill all of each other's needs, that they can be everything to each other. eliminating the necessary roles others must play. Friends, confidants, drinking buddies, sports partners, many people want to assume all these roles for their loved one. Trying to attain this level of dependence stems from the belief that only through neediness would someone choose to be with them. They want to become part and parcel of each other, to meld or merge with that person, to achieve a single entity. "Until we two are one," is a favorite romantic notion worshipped in popular songs and culture.

To me, that sounds bizarre. I find myself wondering what happened to the other person, or who gave up what to be with whom. Did each give up half so that the two of them together become a whole? And which half was given up, the bottom or top? If it was the complete person the other fell in love with, and one of them gives that up, then who is the loved one? Likewise, how much can you love if less of you is there to love? What kind of partner would want you to be less than you are in order to be lovable?

If two people get together, the sum total ought to equal a minimum of two, more, perhaps, if both bring out the best in each other, creating larger "Ones." The purpose of a relationship is to build a place in which you can express yourself completely, aiding your individual growth, which at the same time builds the relationship. Any relationship that starts off with the intention of being anything less than that is surely doomed.

A truly intimate relationship is sacred. At its best, it can be a mirror, held up to show you yourself, both warts and beauty marks; it can be a therapist, working with you to help you free yourself of troublesome emotional baggage; it can be the Red Cross, allowing you to experience the joy of giving without expecting reward.

All people, from infants to the elderly, require intimacy. Yet, for myriad reasons, relatively few succeed in achieving it consistently. Some associate intimacy with engulfment, controlling behavior, dependency, helplessness, or surrendering. These are passive feelings, feelings of being at the mercy of someone else or manipulated. "If I tell him that, then he'll have something he can use against me," is a common belief. "I'll lose my identity if I let her in," is another.

What these voices echo are common experiences of previously unpleasant intimacy, or perceived intimacy. While they may have thought they were being intimate, the truth is they were probably involved with demanding, controlling, dependent, manipulative, dominant people whom they allowed to strip their identity. They experienced what they believed was intimacy. In a truly intimate relationship, however, one's sense of self is enhanced not diminished, encouraged not discouraged, supported not destroyed, nurtured not belittled. Intimacy is synonymous with growth.

So what, then, is intimacy? How do we define it?

Intimacy is a basic human desire. It is the need for relatedness with others, as well as with one's self. Its absence engenders considerable anguish, leaving feelings of emptiness and rejection. Ironically, when the need for intimacy is not met, it leaves us both searching for and fearing it.

Intimacy is a feeling, an experience. It is not an act, although acting out intimacy through various means of expression can be a manifestation of intimacy. The first does not necessarily imply the second. One can act intimately but not feel intimate. There are many people, manipulators, who have learned very well how to fake intimacy (see pseudointimacy, discussed later). They have practiced the words and the style. They've learned what men and women want. But they play the game only to get what they want, not to nourish the relationship. And what they want may be simply the power to control another.

Intimacy allows you to get to know another person completely. And, conversely, it means allowing the second person to know you completely. Intimacy can also be felt for one's self, when a self-exploration without obstacles takes place. It is a willingness to become familiar with another's innermost feelings, no matter how scary or revealing. While there are degrees of intimacy, how intimate you become is contingent on your involvement and willingness to become involved. Different types of relationships demand or require different degrees of intimacy. For example, roommates generally want something less than complete intimacy; permanent mates try to shoot for the moon. One major reason for the breakup of relationships is that the partners each want different degrees of intimacy, one wanting a lot, the other something less.

People who lacked intimacy as children often feel that they were undeserving of it; if they would have been lovable, they think, they would have been loved.

Other children are punished for their expressions of intimacy. After sharing their feelings, their openness, warmth and caring, their childlike innocence, they are confronted by parents, who themselves deprived of intimacy as children, are unable to return the joy in kind. They teach the children that such vulnerabilities are wrong. These children, in turn, eventually learn to fear intimacy.

Still other children learn, through demand or example, that intimacy involves a loss of self-respect, identity and autonomy: You do what you are told or else you are unworthy.

These people, as adults, seek mates who, like their parent(s), withhold affection and are unobtainable. In their efforts to receive the love they missed as children, they choose mates who act the same as their parents. They become very much like children. The doomed behavior repeats itself incessantly. Compelled by past experiences to try to complete their primary relationships with others who are unwilling or unable to give them what they need, these people unconsciously seek to avoid relationships with people who do offer warmth and tenderness. While they actually want and crave intimacy, they associate it with engulfment, abandonment, and criticism. Fearing those feelings, not the intimacy itself, they avoid intimacy. Unless corrected, the cycle remains permanently stuck on "unsatisfied."

Let me give you a powerful example of how some past trauma, either forgotten or buried, can unconsciously affect our current behavior. A thrity-five-year-old woman had been my patient for several weeks, during which time we discussed issues unrelated to her romantic life. She happened to mention casually that she was beginning to panic about a budding relationship. She had been on only one date with this particular man, whom she described as being "very nice, bright, good looking, responsive, all that good stuff," everything she believed she wanted in a man.

"I feel myself starting to let my guard down and wanting to be in a relationship with him, and I know that, after one date, it's too soon to be feeling this way. And in fact, I shouldn't be getting involved at all," she complained. She then tried to skip back and pick up where we'd left off the previous session, on a topic quite unrelated to her romantic life. I was intrigued as much by the cavalier way she'd tried to dismiss her feelings as by what she'd said. The intensity of her anxiety seemed to exceed by a far measure the uncomplicated thoughts she'd related.

I asked her how often this sort of anxiety occured and, prompted by her response, decided we ought to focus on what causes her to panic. "Every time I start to like a guy I get this way," she said.

I asked her to describe exactly what happens.

"I always want to know when he's going to see me again," she said. "If he doesn't tell me right then when we'll go out again, or if he doesn't call me right away, I start to wonder: what's wrong with me?"

Well, of course, there are many (sometimes silly) reasons why this man, or any man, she dated wouldn't call her right away. He may not have liked her car, her house, her smile; she may have made too much money for him or not enough money; he may have thought she didn't like him; he may himself be scared about getting involved with someone; or he may not move at the same pace she does. But she would immediately begin to question herself, always putting the blame on what she imagined to be her own inadequacies or faults.

Compounding this phenomenon was her guilt or ambivalence over having slept with the man, whoever he was; she always initiated sex with her dates the first time out.

I inquired about her relationship with her father, who had been deceased since she was a little girl. On this particular occasion, she seemed more sensitive about the inquiry than usual, a good clue for me that my intuition might be correct. She related for the first time the circumstances of his death.

He had died when she was ten, on the afternoon of the morning of their first angry words ever. While she was at school, he had a heart attack. She never saw him alive again.

As an adult, every time she met a man she liked the unconscious fear that he would leave her, as her father did, surfaced. Every time her guard dropped, her repressed anxiety returned. Whenever a man left her house, the terrible images of her father leaving home for the last time created strong feelings of inadequacy. Her question to men, "Are you going to call me back?" was in truth a metaphor with the message, "Daddy, are you coming back?" And her lingering guilt about not kissing him goodby, "Why wasn't I affectionate with him?" caused her to sleep with every man on the first date. In her mind, it might be the last time she saw him (as her father), and she didn't want daddy to go unkissed ever again.

While learning from familial experiences that intimacy is either a negative emotion or one to be rejected, society tells us that intimacy is something to seek and cherish. That, coupled with one's inherent need for intimacy, leads many people to seek instant intimacy, intimacy without commitment. This is, of course, a contradiction; there can be no intimacy without commitment. Another ironic contradiction: the word commitment itself carries a negative connotation. In this age of so-called personal freedom, commitment is often viewed as imprisonment, implying a loss of freedom. Commitment, in an interpersonal sense, refers to dedication, continuity, conviction, constancy. When we are committed to an ideal we maintain a strong belief, one that is meant to endure over time, one that transcends whimsy.

Since the advent of the birth control pill, which preceded other social factors responsible for a mass change in attitude, so-called instant intimacy has taken the form of sexuality. Sex feels like intimacy. It is warm and close, with physical contact that seems like nurturing. Such encounters offer, to those experiencing problems with intimacy, a form of short-term closeness without confronting the anxiety of a long term relationship. But as you may have experienced, sex without love (or at least without intimacy) isn't tremendously satisfying. At its best, it can feel good as long as it lasts and can be a pleasant physical release. At its worst, it can magnify feelings of self-loathing. Despite the contact with another body, eventually the loneliness can't be hidden anymore.

Now, as more people necessarily fret over contracting sexually transmitted diseases, quick fixes of intimacy through sex are not as attractive as they once were; those concerned have to look elsewhere for their doses of intimacy. But whether it's the fear of AIDS or an inability to hide the loneliness anymore, most people eventually look for true intimacy.

Self-Intimacy

Just as you cannot truly love another if you do not first love yourself, intimacy between two people cannot exist unless both know themselves intimately. Self-intimacy sets the foundation for intimacy with others. There are cases in which intimacy with others has served to foster self-intimacy, though generally the reverse is true. Self-intimacy refers to you knowing yourself; getting in touch with both your positive and negative thoughts, fantasies, and so on. The more you learn about yourself, the more you can share, and thus, the more intimacy is possible.

Equally as important, self-exploration in the area of intimacy allows you to sense when it's not there. It enables you to distinguish between pseudointimacy and the real thing. Those feelings of nonengagement, alienation and estrangement, common in previous relationships, become knowable once you become self-intimate. And in that way, you can actually seek to correct them, to become more intimate with yourself and others.

Becoming Intimate

Before any intimacy is achieved between people, both partners must be willing to be intimate. "You will be intimate with me," is a demand unlikely to be heeded. Without mutual consent, either implied or stated, no real intimacy can occur. That doesn't mean, of course, that both people have to feel as strongly about intimacy, because the momentum of a flowering relationship is not always felt simultaneously by each partner. In general, there must be at least an inclination to accept intimacy as a goal, a willingness for it to be a possibility.

Out of that willingness, the partners must establish an atmosphere of openness, each person exploring the sensations of closeness. This getting-to-know process occurs when each person lets down initial defenses. As familiarity increases, and a feeling of sharing takes place, further closeness occurs. This sets the stage for dialogues and deeper sharing, the expression of innermost thoughts and wishes.

At this point, it is not uncommon for these people to feel and admit that they've never voiced such honest words to anyone ever before. If they have done so, it probably feels different. Each has given up a part of self to the other and has received, in kind, a similar gift. There is the implicit understanding that it is given safely, that the trust will not be violated. The acceptance of the disclosure increases the desire to reveal more, and, in a wonderfully self-propelling spiral, the bond between them solidifies, further increasing the desire to disclose more.

In theory, the evloving process of true intimacy continues unendingly. In reality complex emotions and subconscious motivations often hinder the process, and indeed, subvert the relationship itself.

When a relationship is new and the uniqueness of it makes each moment seem as if life's possibilities are endless, the thought of having to work to maintain intimacy seems ludicrous. Intoxicated by the romance, the partners believe, "I'll always feel this way." Yet eventually, in even the most passionate romances, one or both partners becomes accustomed to the feeling, making it only the common level of reality. And, unless the mates find a way to keep their communication one step ahead of the reality, to nourish their intimacy, the relationship may suffer or even extinguish.

Openness

Openness is essential for maintaining an intimate relationship. Openness is an atmosphere in which two lovers are allowed to breathe, feeling free to be themselves, whether that Self is expressed through silence or conversation.

Openness always implies trust, which evolves spontaneously, without demand that it be there or criticisms of its absence, when both lovers feel secure that their integrity will remain safe. However, trust does not always imply openness; like pseudointimacy, there is also pseudo-openness.

Mutual respect for the individuality and freedom of the other is an absolute prerequisite for openness, even if that individuality manifests as a difference of opinion. People do have their differences. Trying to force both to feel and think the same automatically precludes openness. Some lovers feel threatened when their partners disagree with them. They will either change their own point of view or try to get the other to change, in the mistaken belief that complete harmony is necessary.

Well, the former action only indicates an insecurity, a desire to subsume the self to save the relationship, which probably dooms it anyway. The latter indicates a domineering personality, also insecure, which can't tolerate a personality that isn't a direct extension of itself.

In an atmosphere of true openness, there is no need or desire to infringe on the freedoms and individuality of the other partner. Each person recognizes that it was an individual with whom they fell in love, and an individual with whom they want to remain in love.

Self-revelation

Openness can also be expressed through self-revelation, which is a willingness to share actively with your partner the conflicting or sensitive aspects of your nature. This allows your partner to participate in your life, to come to know you fully.

There are, unfortunately, many people who are pleased to share the happy or positive sides of your nature but who want to run away or discount the stunning conflicts you may harbor. One patient of mine fell in love with a woman who told him, right from the beginning of their relationship, that she suffered from powerful emotional problems and was subject to dark moods. She felt obliged to warn him, in case he felt he would be unable to deal with them. If so, she said, she would understand his inability, but she didn't want to invest any more heart in him if that were so.

Although he heard her words, he treated them lightly, being so caught up in the wonderful energy of their new relationship. He quieted her repeated warnings with the assurance that he was different than other men, and would be there with her through thick and thin.

A month or so down the line, she lapsed into a moody, almost catatonic spell and needed support from him. He became shaken by the sight of this woman, whom he had known to be only strong and cheerful, and he was unable to offer the assistance he had guaranteed. Having had no experience with emotional problems, he found himself completely unprepared for the reality. He disappeared, more or less, for the two weeks in which her dour mood hung over her, unrelentingly, like a swarm of insects. And finally, when it ceased and she became again the woman he'd fallen in love with, he visited her only to break the relationship officially.

For her, the official break-up was superfluous; the relationship had already been violated by his broken promises. Never before had she offered to let anyone view her dark side, but buoyed by his apparently unwavering love and commitment, she let down her resistance. She was shattered by the disappointing experience; never again, she resolved, would she allow a man to get that close to her.

While an extreme example, this story illustrates that self-revelation, without mutual readiness, can be destructive. Self-revelation makes you vulnerable, and more, it places the other person in a unique position.

Start slowly. Pay attention to any clues offered. Do take chances, of course, but be as certain as you can that your disclosures will be accepted. If you do offer them despite clues to the contrary—if you ignore evidence that indicates such disclosures will not be received well—you are in effect dumping your problem on another who is unready for it. Just because readiness doesn't occur when you think it should doesn't mean it won't as the relationship develops.

Self-revelation requires the utmost sensitivity. Rushing into it too soon may be damaging to the relationship in the long run. It takes some people longer than others to be ready to hear what might be construed as bad news. Just because someone says or hints that they aren't ready in the first week doesn't mean that in the second, third or fourth weeks the situation won't change. In fact, people who know themselves well enough and are honest enough to say "not yet" about their readiness or willingness to hear your disclosures often become the most intimate; they first want to be certain of a mutual commitment.

Self-revelation or self-disclosure is an astonishingly beautiful way to nourish intimacy, to raise it to increasingly higher levels. In relationships based on intimacy, openness and closeness, these revealing communications are offered, accepted and reciprocated. They may be joyful, embarrassing or painful, but all are honest and contribute to the relationship by continuing to expand the atmosphere of trust.

After moments of deep honest communication, the feeling of intimacy produced often leads to its highest physical expression, which feels all the more stupendous because of the emotional connection.

Unfortunately, knowing that such closeness often leads to sex, there are some people who intentionally violate the emotional, and physical, privacy of needy partners by feigning intimacy in order to get what they want. They engage in the physical expression of intimacy without feeling intimate. They may even delude themselves into believing that, because they act intimately, they are intimate. In fact, both partners may be party to the charade in order to justify a passionate, stormy romance. They play at intimacy in order to ward off real intimacy.

Pseudointimacy

These people know the words their partners want to hear without feeling the meaning themselves. They have learned how to behave intimately, but without the genuine commitment. What results is pseudointimacy, not the real thing. And someone—it's not hard to figure out whom— usually gets badly hurt. But in the final analysis, the real loser is the one who lacks the ability to share genuinely and openly.

Pseudointimacy, or instant intimacy, does not always have to be intentionally manufactured. It also refers to those relationships that occur when two, often needy, people come together and feel, for whatever reasons, that they've known each other much longer than they have. This usually occurs in such confined places as airplanes, ocean cruises and even cocktail parties. Having met in a special, contained environment, they develop an unnaturally quick intimacy by sharing a great deal in their short time together. As a consequence, they feel close and the vibes are magically sensuous. But when the trip or party ends, they invariably withdraw into their former selves, sometimes laden with guilt that they've shared too much too soon. The next time they meet, if there is a next time, they feel uncomfortable in each other's presence and probably embarrassed. And, should they attempt to recapture what was, they fail miserably.

In a vacuum, pseudointimacy can be quite a delightful experience. It feels good, is a great way to pass the time, and can even lead to ecstatic love making. Problems arise only when both partners are unaware of what has happened and begin to expect too much. Just as even a greasy hamburger tastes great when you're famished, pseudointimacy feels wonderful when you're needy. The moral is that the true deliciousness of a hamburger should not be judged after a long fast, and conclusions about the genuine intimacy of a relationship must not be reached during periods of critical need and want. Remember the phrase, "On the rebound."

Genuine intimacy takes time to develop and can only do so through the repeated sharing of feelings, thoughts and ideas. The pains and pleasures brought to the relationship by each party must be expressed by both partners, and there must be time for them to develop. Certainly, genuine intimacy can result from such beginnings, but care must be exercised to recognize the relationship for exactly what it is: a beginning.

Maintaining an Intimate Relationship

In my role as a marriage counselor, I listen to a host of complaints, most of them revolving somehow around communication, or the lack of it. And what my experience has told me is that a good relationship isn't necessarily judged by the number of conflicts a couple has, or the severity of them, but by how these conflicts are resolved.

Previous generations resolved most conflicts by power: the husband was the dominant partner, the wife subservient; so the decision was made unilaterally. With more relationships based on intimacy rather than role, new approaches have become necessary, particularly since the women's movement. Two-breadwinner families are now the norm and not the exception. Rejecting traditional roles and traditional interpersonal expectations, couples struggle to find ways of dealing with the various issues that arise. Differences of opinion, division of chores, opposing styles and beliefs, are common sources of conflict.

In my experience, the most effective tool to resolve such conflicts is borrowed from the business world: negotiation. While it may seem foreign to negotiate points in your relationship, just as if you were working out a contract, the positive results are indisputable.

People who have developed a degree of intimacy often feel—wrongly—that their partners ought to be able to read their minds. So, when the trash begins to accumulate and stink up the kitchen because each partner assumed the other was going to take it out, fighting may escalate, not because of the single unimportant issue, but because it symbolizes expectations and assumptions. "Well," says the husband, "I assumed you'd do it because . . ." "Why me?" the wife asks. "Why do you expect me to do it? Who do you think I am?"

I have taught couples to sit down, legal pad in hand, and work out a contract for the terms of their relationship, everything from who takes out the trash to how the finances are to be handled and who balances the checkbook, from child-rearing duties to child-rearing philosophy.

If each partner gives up something to get something in return—"I'll do this if you do that"—neither gets everything wanted, nor does either one feel taken advantage of. At the same time, both partners know exactly what's expected of them and what they can expect of the other. The rules are posted, so to speak, in black and white; misunderstandings are cut to a minimum.

There are some partners who initially handle the negotiations like spoiled children, sulking, throwing tantrums, and storming out of the room when they don't get exactly their way. Others exercise power plays, using money or sex to enhance their positions. Eventually, the negotiating process teaches a kind of acceptance that infiltrates their consciousness.

Once a couple learns how to negotiate, each partner feels more confident in the ability to maintain individuality and harmony in the relationship. Often, in fact, the negotiating becomes a microcosm of the relationship, and turns out to be bigger than the points being negotiated. The negotiating itself becomes a heady experience, enjoyed by the partners. Some couples even schedule regular business meetings in order to help further their intimacy and understanding. Using this approach allows them to handle the larger, more emotional, conflicts without intense fighting.

Couples who negotiate, in my opinion, are committed to each other and to improving their relationships. They value trust, mutual respect and the integrity and feelings of their mate.

Compromise and Accommodation

In negotiations, you must learn to distinguish between compromise and accommodation. In accommodation, one person gives up a position in order to accommodate or appease the other. While this may sound like a perfect way to keep the peace, my experience has shown me that doing so generally builds up resentment in the person doing the accommodating. Eventually, that resentment builds to the boiling point, and the person erupts uncontrollably: "After all I've done for you . . .."

If not in a single eruption, then the resentment will invariably eke out indirectly. A suddenly irrational statement, directed at the accommodated person, or a profoundly nasty mood, may be traced back to a series of accommodations. Gradually (or not so gradually, with some people) there is an erosion of respect for the accommodated by the accommodator who feels that no mutuality exists in the relationship.

Compromise, on the other hand, allows each partner to express an individual position. If there can be no clear agreement drawn after the presentations, they then look for a third option. "I want a blue couch in the living room," says the man adamantly. "But I want a white one," says the woman, equally adamant. The solution? A third color entirely or submission of the final decision to an impartial third party.

In relationships, when people are stubborn, the underlying message is "I must have my way—or else."

Often the issue being articulated has nothing to do with the true motivation for the declaration. It may, in fact, have something to do with another issue that's too volatile or too sensitive to be discussed. It may even be redirected resentment being expressed by an habitual accommodator.

Particularly with macho men or macha women, giving in or compromising on a point is associated with a loss of self-esteem. They fear that if they don't maintain their ground at all times, they'll be thought of as weak.

In intimate relationships, stubbornness has no value at all. It only serves to create distance, tension and anxiety. If, in what you believe to be an open and intimate relationship, you find yourself constantly engaged in stubborn battles for turf, examine your motives to decide whether you are truly involved in an intimate relationship and whether you truly want to be. In short, stubbornness is a signal of trouble in the relationship.

Anger

Passion being a component of most intimate relationships, emotions will occasionally run high. Tempers will flare, and anger will be expressed. Relationships in which the partners claim never to argue, or indeed never argue, must, in my opinion, lack passion. And without passion, even intimacy can be boring.

One couple with whom my wife and I were friendly a few years ago seemed, on the surface, to be perfect: always sweet and loving and never, they claimed, argumentative. Our friends in common looked on them with a mixture of awe and admiration. But I was suspicious. ("You're always suspicious," my wife told me; we argued.) Of course, it came as a great shock to almost everyone—

but not me——when they announced their plans to divorce. "We just fell out of love," the husband claimed.

Sure, it's possible that they did fall out of love. And sure, it's possible for there to be relationships which aren't battered about by anger from time to time. But I suspect that their absence of anger indicated a lack of passion for each other.

Certainly, I'm not implying that knock-down drag-out fights are healthy. They're not and are probably indicative of some severe emotional conflicts. Yet in an intimate relationship, two separate but equal partners are bound to step on each other's toes once in a while.

How they deal with that anger, not the frequency of conflicts, indicates the health of their relationship. Telling your partner that you're angry and why is important. Pouting or withholding anger is childish and counterproductive. One of my pet peeves is being told by my wife, in response to my question, that nothing is wrong, even though I can plainly see that something is bothering her. She holds her chin in a very distinctive way when she is angry and trying not to show it.

The withholding of anger is generally meant to be punishment (as if not expressing it hurts anyone but the withholder). Some people just don't want to let go of their anger, because, in a slightly perverse way, it feels good, it feels comfortable. They may have been brought up, as many of us were, to hide our true feelings. We were taught to repress our anger, that displaying the emotion is bad.

Nothing could be further from the truth. Just as pain is a symptom of possible physiological problems, anger symbolizes emotional distress. Ignoring it and repressing it do nothing at all, except to squirt it out more destructively in other, more surprising, directions.

If your aims are to be heard and then to resolve the issue, pick an appropriate time to express your anger. While your wife's at work, surrounded by a dozen co-workers, isn't the time to call her on the phone to say you're pissed off about what she said to you at dinner last night. Tonight's dinner would be much more appropriate.

It always helps to start the conversation by saying, "I want to tell you how I feel. I feel _____ when you say or do _____" Keep it specific and try not to bring up how he forgot about your birthday fourteen years ago. It's your fault you've been harboring that for fourteen years. Talk about how you feel, because no one can argue with your feelings; they're your feelings.

In most intimate relationships, the partners try to avoid hurting each other's feelings. By putting it on that level, and not pointing fingers, resolution comes quicker and is more satisfying.

If your aim isn't to be heard, but simply to vent or dump your uncomfortable feelings, be aware that resolution of the problem isn't likely; escalation is. Whatever caused you to be angry is one thing; how you express it is another matter entirely. You have no license to say anything you want, under the pretense of getting it off your chest, unless you plan to pay the price. You have a responsibility to your partner, and if you feel that you've been wronged, wronging back is not the solution. Sure, just letting it all hang out feels great sometimes, but it doesn't come free. Just as you justified your emotional free-for-all by what was said or done, don't you think your partner will do the same, feeling justified by your outburst?

Equally important as communicating your anger in a constructive manner is learning to listen to your partner's anger constructively. That means listening openly, not defensively. Defensive listening isn't listening at all, it's only waiting to talk. And when you do—usually to say, "Not me, I didn't do that"—your partner's anger will be multiplied by the force of your denials. It matters little whether the anger is, in your mind, legitimate or justified; after all, it's not your anger. Your job is to hear how your partner is feeling. That's all.

To understand your partner's feeling without reacting similarly is a sign of maturity and self-confidence. You don't have to accept blame, even if your partner's anger is aimed at you. Most of the time, just listening and accepting blame *if you deserve it*, will defuse the anger. Having been allowed to vent feelings without reprimands, your partner will feel good about the relationship. And so should you.

Part II

Real People

"Where are all the good men (or women)?" they ask constantly. All of the people you are about to meet ask the same question at some point during the course of their psychotherapy with me. These are real people just like you, with real concerns, and real struggles. You might recognize yourself in one or more of these people. The issues they face and are dealing with are not uncommon. They are presented here because it is often easier to recognize the difficulties others face than it is our own. Their weaknesses and shortcomings are our weaknesses and shortcomings. You might see solutions and alternatives that could apply to you. That is the most important reason for including their stories.

The Sophisticated Adolescent
Business is Business and Romance is Romance

Donna represents the young woman of the 1990s. In her business world she is definitely a nineties woman, but in her dating life, she is a girl of the fifties. As you read Donna's story, pay attention to how her values developed through the profound impact of her home environment, and the values of her parents. This is an excellent example of how sexism in the home contributes to your self-worth and self-concept.

Donna lived in two worlds. In some ways you could say that she was two people. She tried to adapt to the conflicting demands of her two roles and her conflicting desire to please her family and herself. Her solution is a common one, despite its ineffectiveness in bringing her happiness. Until she focused on the issues, she felt doomed to merely repeat the old patterns. Through the process of self-examination, reinforced by action, she was eventually able to see more options and make better choices.

Donna

Donna was thirty-three years old when I first met her. A highly successful executive headhunter, she was a dynamo of will and strength on the job, yet when it came to romance she would suddenly assume the personality of a giggling sixteen-year-old. She moved with ease through a man's world as long as the relationship was business. The moment the prospect of dating and love appeared, she felt she had to subjugate her intelligence and become inferior, believing unconsciously but firmly that the proper female role is to be subservient to men.

Donna came from an upper middle-class home in which her tradition-minded parents stressed the importance of education. The idea was firmly implanted in her that she should grow up to be a wife, and that she not have a career. Despite that, she vowed not to become a housewife like her mother and set out to prove herself the equal of men, earning an M.B.A. from a prestigious university. A hard worker who relied on her bright mind, articulate tongue, and winning personality to succeed in business, she achieved her goal, and was considered the consummate professional by all of her associates and clients.

An attractive woman, Donna enjoyed being the center of attention wherever she went. She dressed well, drove exotic cars, surrounded herself in luxury. Her many hobbies included dancing, tennis, gymnastics, playing the piano, and reading romance novels.

Donna dated often, but rarely the same man more than a few times. Her inability to find a fulfilling relationship resulted, in part, from her sudden and inexplicable reversion to adolescent behavior, shyness, demureness, stuttering, indecisiveness, whenever she sensed romance possible. Although such actions represented the diametric opposite of everything she believed in, she was actually unaware of the syndrome.

When Donna first came to me, her favorite phrase was, "Why don't you set me up with . . .?"

I asked her how she met the men she dates. "I usually ask my friends to set me up with somebody," she said. "That's the best way."

I asked her where she looks for men on her own. "I'm always looking," she said. "When I go to the gas station, I sometimes talk to the guy getting gas. I might even talk to the attendant. I'm always out there."

My response to Donna was, "You're fishing for trout in a toilet." Why? Because she didn't seem to care who the man was or where he was, just so long as it was a male. She believed that sort of behavior qualifies as networking, as being "out there."

I asked her if, in her capacity as an executive head-hunter, she hands out her business card to gas station attendants, supermarket checkers, and taxicab drivers. "Of course not," she said, clearly puzzled by my question. "I hand them out to professional people."

"You only hand out your card," I said, "where you'll likely increase your business?"

"That's right."

"Then why don't you do the same with romance?"

That conclusion may seem obvious enough to you, but Donna had never thought of romance in those terms. She operated under the notion that business is business and should be taken seriously, and romance is romance and should be taken lightly.

As with most of us, business was something Donna learned as an adult, unencumbered by any previous mind-sets. However, when it came to romance and love, the images of childhood fantasies and stories still maintained an influence over her adult thinking, if only because years of repetition created belief systems which do not dissipate easily or completely.

Donna's ideas about business weren't formed through television, movies and books, or, if they were, what she learned about it through those sources was that business has to be taken seriously. What she learned from those sources about romance was that it is all sweetness and light. Hence the disparity between her two selves. These archaic, primitive, childhood lessons have been transmitted from culture to culture, over generations, without refinements.

The strength of Donna's belief that business and pleasure should not mix in any sense also prevented men with whom she worked from asking her to go on dates. Her emotional undercurrent, of which she was unaware, quickly imparted the message to men, who would have otherwise been attracted to her, that she was strictly off-limits. She was seemingly so concerned with ethics, morality and appearing competent, that she discarded her humanity.

Mindless Mate-Searching

Such a splitting was so strong in Donna that she left even her normally powerful intellect at home when looking for a mate. She would really have liked to find a doctor, a lawyer, a dentist, a professional man, but she went to the wrong places. The chance of locating a doctor on a bar stool seems remote at best (that doesn't mean doctors don't go to bars, it means simply that if a doctor was who she really wanted, she needed to refine the focus of her search). She claimed she wanted a man with a sense of humor, someone who was psychologically minded, intelligent, financially successful, sensual, sexual, and affectionate, but she settled for any man at all.

Given her proclivities, how many of Donna's budding romances do you think reached fruition?

Donna's belief system said that men only want a particular type of woman, a woman who fits a specific bill of fare. So she lied about her age, pretending she was under thirty; she played down her intelligence, because she had been taught that men don't like intelligent women; she showed herself to be helpless, because she believed men like that. The basic contradiction in effect here was that she behaved in ways, and looked in places, which would surely fail to attract (except by accident) the type of man she truly wanted, or thought she wanted.

When she did attract a man who would open doors for her and want to take care of her like a China doll, he was usually twenty years her senior, a man who came of age during the 1950s. Just as if it were a puzzle, the pieces which comprised motivation and action fit together beautifully: Donna was really searching for someone like Ricky Nelson, the way he appeared on "Ozzie and Harriet," because he was the romantic idol she idealized most as a child. She placed onto this Ricky stick figure all the thoughts, notions and preconceptions she had ever learned about romance.

The irony, you understand, is that these men she dated, whether they were older or even of the same general age, tended to make her feel stifled. She had fantasies of being with her ideal, yet she really couldn't stand him when she met him. Even if she hadn't left him first, as her natural strength of will and opinionated nature eventually surfaced, he would have turned off, finding that she was not the woman he originally met.

Donna the Professional or Donna the Date?

During the self-inventory, it became obvious that Donna saw herself in two distinct ways: Donna the professional and Donna the date. Her sense of splitting between the two was extreme. As a professional, she listed herself as intelligent, attractive, a good dresser, contemporary, financially successful, professional, outgoing and independent.

But when it came to Donna the date, she listed herself as honest, understanding, dependent, conservative, neat and having somewhat of a sense of humor.

Rating her ideal mate, Donna listed him as being intelligent, attractive, a good dresser, successful, outgoing, independent, sexual, generous, understanding and psychologically oriented. In her mind, Donna the date and her ideal mate coincided well enough to make a successful match.

The discrepancy and moment of realization came when Donna saw how her friends had described her. Each one had rated her, overall, as being intelligent, attractive, a good dresser, contemporary, financially successful, professional, outgoing, playful, sexual and funny. In other words, they saw her not as the little girl who succumbs and reverts to a giggling teenager, but as the mature, capable and exciting professional. Yet, those who had seen her before with her dates listed someone else entirely: clingy, deferent, silly, immature, nonassertive, reserved, passive and coy.

Exploring the Discrepancy. Presented with this jarring information, a wide chasm obviously existing between her self-perception and those of people she trusted, Donna began to explore the hidden meaning behind the discrepancy, as well as its manifestations in her personality on a day-to-day basis. Part of the exploration led her to understand that she was behaving with her dates in the same manner that she had behaved in high school and college.

What had been apparent to everyone else, and indeed even to Donna on some level as she made two lists of herself, was that she possessed, in effect, two different personalities. The intense moment of awakening, the realization or enlightenment, that took place when she noted the true extent of her splitting allowed her to view her actions much more objectively. To her astonishment, she saw that Donna the executive had not been integrated emotionally or psychologically into Donna the social being.

As she herself admitted after the exercise, one of the consequences of this splitting was that she would choose arenas for trying to find men that were appropriate only for a teenager, not an adult; that it was Donna the teenager making the choices of where to go, where to meet men and how to behave, not the competent professional. So, in hoping to meet a man in places like gas stations and supermarkets, and automatically eliminating the generous supply of compatible professional men with whom she worked, Donna was relying on a selection process that works only when the quality of the mate is not a criterion, for example, when a teenager is out body hunting.

What Donna learned was that she tended to leave the best part of herself, the modern woman, back in the office while the teenager went out to meet men. She realized that the woman in the office also had to go out on that date, in order to moderate the teenager's childish actions.

Of course, everyone at different times becomes appropriately a combination of child, teenager and adult.

We call on the child when we allow ourselves to have fun and experience the small pleasures of life; the teenager, for most of us, represents an awakening sexuality, lust, hormonal instincts, and so on; and the adult is the rational being. Each softens, refines or complements the others.

During office meetings, a professional usually subordinates childlike feelings in order to get the job done efficiently. Later, during a business discussion over drinks, subordination is of the teenage self, which may be demanding sexual consummation when that, too, would be inappropriate.

By the same token, when work is completed and fun and pleasure are in order, the professional may call upon the playfulness of the child and the sexuality of the teenager.

Naturally, combinations of these three, vying for attention at various intensities, cause different people to manifest different personalities. None of them completely precludes the others. A business executive may indeed allow his spontaneity and playfulness to surface, just so long as his decisions are not ruled by the child. Similarly, a personnel choice ruled by the teenager is not likely to be made with the success of the company in mind.

Because the acceptability of being a professional on a date was in question to her, the concept seeming so alien, Donna had to do a bit of homework. I needed to demonstrate to her that professional women do not have to abandon their competence the moment they leave the boardroom; that they do not, in social situations, have to become children. I asked her to pay closer attention to professional females she knew who had been successful in both business and interpersonal relationships.

In truth, Donna had noticed many such women over the years, but the considerations planted in her mind as a young girl watching television programs like *Father Knows Best* and *Ozzie and Harriet* mutated those impressions and repainted them to reflect the idea that, to succeed with men, women had to resort to silliness. What we had her do, by studying reality more carefully, was create a new database of images that allowed her to feel that women could be as competent, mature and intelligent in the dining room or bedroom as in the boardroom. The goal was to reintegrate her two selves: make the date more adult, and the businesswoman softer.

The Plan Worked

I asked her to expand her reading diet of trade journals, trash novels (which generally present romances in which the female is helpless and subservient), and women's issues to include anything that might possibly interest her on any other level. By emphasizing different aspects of her personality, she would, I hoped, reawaken the child inside, causing her to present a lighter-hearted face to the world. On the job, where she had always been unremittingly stern, keeping her personal life so secretive and segregated that no one with whom she worked even knew if she was married, she would be able to inject some warmth and fun.

The plan worked, and Donna began sharing selected details with her colleagues. Soon she was able to introduce a little humor, allowing her natural wit and charm to show. In time, she cast aside much of the masculine persona she had thought women needed in order to succeed.

The time came to actively seek out mates. Previously, she had relied only on girlfriends and serendipity to find her dates. Whenever the supply of men referred by her friends dried up, she had taken to the streets, approaching anyone. Now, having decided to approach the situation less haphazardly, she began to include the people she should have included all along: her co-workers, with whom she had everything in common. Performing her work duties, Donna was often in social situations for business purposes with men who, if they weren't right for her themselves, might have been in a position to know someone who was.

Slowly, painfully at first, then with increasing facility, she began to open up to them, revealing the full extent of her personality. And that included her marital status; yes, she told them, she was in the market. Interestingly, opening up her personality had the side benefit of increasing her business. As she became more integrated, she was more fun to be with and, consequently, attracted more clients, some of whom had been previously scared away by her apparently solitary dimension.

Besides her colleagues and clients, Donna also eventually worked up the courage to share her search with others; it got easier, she said, the more she put herself out there. She spoke with her gynecologist, who was a single woman about Donna's age, and her dentist, whose offer once before to fix her up with his nephew was summarily rejected. Isn't it interesting how Donna, and she's certainly representative of the majority, had been willing to let her dentist and gynecologist explore her most intimate body cavities without embarrassment yet was unwilling to let them know she was single and available?

Besides enlisting these people as agents, Donna decided to match her athletic talents with her desire to meet a professional man: she joined a tennis club in an affluent area of town. She also bought herself a good bicycle and joined a cycling club, going on long weekend rides. Additionally, owing to her business bent, she joined two local chambers of commerce, which netted her four or five potential mates and perhaps another half dozen solid business contacts.

A couple years after doing the program, while attending a Christmas party given by one of her clients, the chief executive officer of a medium-sized corporation, Donna found out that he had been interested in dating her for well over a year. He said he was surprised that she accepted his offer to attend the party, considering that she had turned him down on similar invitations several times before.

She never turned him down again. Donna is married now, with a child and a thriving business.

Discoveries

All's well that ends well. Donna went on an inner journey that changed her life. She took risks, experimented with new behaviors, challenged old beliefs. Donna's experience forced her to be honest with herself and to recognize that she could combine her personal values with her business acumen. She learned that she did not have to keep the two sides of herself separate. She learned that she did not have to behave like a man in order to function in a man's world, nor did she have to put up with the sexist attitudes generally found in corporate America.

Rather she discovered that, by combining the best of both worlds, she was more powerful and more satisfied. By integrating her personality, she opened new and better options. She didn't have to sacrifice her sense of self to be liked and had even more energy to invest in her world.

Like the woman in the movie *Baby Boom*, Donna discovered that she was even able to run her business to include her family.

L.A. Woman
A Case of Mistaken Assumptions

Vicki represents the woman who believes that "it is not how you feel, but how you look" that really matters. She merely wanted to be seen in all the right places, figuring that she was so "hot" looking that she couldn't miss. In part, Vicki had the right idea; she wanted affluent men, so the places she went catered to the affluent. But she neglected to think that these affluent men may want more than someone who was expert on the latest dirt from *People* magazine. Vicki treated herself like a piece of bait, hoping that fish would come along and take a bite.

Vicki is a product of the media that repeatedly tries to sell us on the idea that if we looked a particular way —wore the right clothes, and went to the right places—we would find happiness. However, the media's only interest is in selling us its products.

Vicki's explorations led her to discover that the men that she wanted to attract have a different set of expectations as to what they wanted in a mate. She came to recognize that the type of men she was interested in would want something more than a well-packaged air-head. They were looking for a partner.

Vicki will take you on her journey of self- transformation. She decides that rather than change her standards for what she wants in a man, she will take the more difficult route; she will change herself. During the course of this transformation, she finds that she could be alone with someone she truly likes: herself.

Vicki

Vicki, twenty-six, was everyone's stereotypical idea of the "L.A. Woman," despite hailing from Buffalo. She changed the color and cut of her hair the way most people change their socks, and she was a certifiable expert on plastic surgery, having had her nose done twice, her breasts implanted, and her chin restructured. She wore a Rolex watch and drove whatever happened to be the trendy car of the moment.

She could recite the name and address of every bar in town yet couldn't remember the names of half of her one-night stands. She claimed to know what every man wanted, but she hadn't had a sustained relationship in more than three years.

Vicki had graduated from high school and worked at odd jobs for two years before attending cosmetology school. She signed up for every self-help group imaginable in the late 1970s, solely to meet men, not to get better, because, in her estimation, she never needed help.

Longing for a Beverly Hills Prince

A hairstylist, Vicki spent her days gossiping, talking about men, fashion, jewelry, Club Med, and the rest. Her dream was to find a prince who would carry her off to his castle in Beverly Hills. To her, these were the important things in life, and because her friends, all single, thought, talked and acted the exact same way, her behavior was reinforced.

All of Vicki's money was spent going to the in places, where, she believed, the wealthier men would see her. She saw herself as hot stuff, and she couldn't understand why Mr. Right hadn't come along.

When I asked her what type of man she wanted and where she went to find him, Vicki could only parrot the words she'd heard fashionable women use to describe their dream lover: "Responsible, reliable, good looking, rich, powerful, someone who treats a lady like a lady." After stammering a long time, she finally conceded that "treating a lady like a lady" meant: buy me, take me, give me.

I asked her where she went to find the men she claimed to want. True to character, she rattled off a list of the city's trendiest bars, wealthiest country clubs, and parties given by name people, some of whom were her clients.

The man Vicki said she wanted might very well have been found at places like those, but Vicki couldn't possibly have landed him. Bluntly speaking, she had the wrong stuff. The type of man she described would have no use for a woman like Vicki, except perhaps as a mistress. Hers was a world of cliches; she didn't have a single original idea in her head, yet she said she was looking for a bright, erudite, sophisticated man. What Vicki really wanted was to walk directly onto the pages of a Judith Krantz or Jackie Collins novel, where she could happily live her life with such men as she described lusting after her, she having something which they wanted and for which they were willing to lay the earth at her feet. She didn't want a relationship, she wanted a fairy tale, someone to rescue her from a life of drudgery.

Vicki wasn't stupid. Unconscious, maybe, but not stupid. In fact, with her quick mind, if she had taken the time to read anything heftier than *TV Guide*, she might have gained some real understanding of the world and been able to meet the type of man she said she wanted.

More than anything else, in this particular area of her life, she was being unrealistic. But that unreality was a protective barrier against her losing her independence. Why? Because, in the back of her mind, she always felt that Mr. Perfect would someday come along. And when he did, the real, objective, unequalled Mr. Perfect, better than any man, she would be ready for him . . . by being Mrs. Perfect.

Absolute Perfection

How she planned to do that was not by cultivating her mind, her sensibilities, or her talents, but through plastic surgery. Vicki believed that her failure to attract Mr. Perfect could be attributed to her physical shortcomings, real and imagined. She thought that if she possessed the features of a movie goddess, she could have her pick of any man in the world. She visualized herself sauntering into a roomful of men, heads turning so quickly to catch a glimpse of her that a chiropractor would be needed. What she didn't include in that mental scene was conversation, or intimacy or caring, not to mention fighting and compromising.

Besides spending every free minute in front of either the bathroom mirror or the one on the gym wall, Vicki submitted to the plastic surgeon's knife at least five times: her nose, her breasts, her legs, her chin, her eyes; all of them were redone to specifications suggested from photographs of famous beautiful women. Each time she had another area done, she truly believed that she became that more much alluring, but she always felt that one more area would need to be done before she reached the pinnacle: Absolute Perfection.

In the self-inventory, Vicki saw herself as God's gift to mankind: gorgeous, funny, exciting, sexy, humorous, interesting and a good dancer. Naturally, her friends tended to corroborate these characteristics.

The problem was, Vicki only knew people who were as vacuous as she. So the fact that they told her she was the wonderful woman she believed herself to be only caused her to wonder why she couldn't land Mr. Perfect, whom she described as being: responsible, reliable, good looking, rich and powerful. That there was a major discrepancy between who she could land and who she wanted to land never occurred to her, because she possessed so little self-knowledge. Had she solicited the opinions of people sufficiently different from her viewpoint and personality, the answer would have become obvious.

The lesson to be learned from Vicki is that important information about oneself can be obtained from the self-inventory, except, in cases like hers, when the so-called objective opinions come from clones of oneself.

In this case, Vicki was lucky enough to have me to intervene. However, anyone outside her circle of friends who knew her reasonably well could have played the same role.

Mistaken Assumptions

No one needs psychological counseling to interpret either the self-inventory or any aspect of this program. The truth is, most people have not usually stopped long enough to evaluate all the facts at hand. If your goal seems to be eluding you, explore objectively all the material and, if you're committed, attack from a different angle. First try it according to your friends' perceptions. If their viewpoints are too congruent with yours, try finding someone whose outlook on life is slightly different. If their descriptions paint you in a light different than yours, their objectivity may be just what you need. If you're failing now in your approach, what have you got to lose?

"Vicki," I asked, "how do you account for the fact that these guys, who you think are so great, don't seem interested in you?"

"I have no idea," she said. She honestly had no idea.

"Well then," I said, "let me offer you several possible explanations. One: They're too messed up to see how wonderful you are." She liked that.

"Two: You're mistaking their wonderfulness." That also was acceptable.

"Three: They're seeing something in you that they're not turned on to." She looked less pleasant.

"Four: You're not who you think you are." Perplexed, now.

"Five: You're representing who you would like to be, not who you are." Astonished.

"Six: What you think these men want isn't what they want."

Vicki stared at me without emotion. I think that, although statements three through six, particularly, had annoyed her, they may also have struck chords of recognition. I explained: She had made assumptions about who these men were, and therefore what they wanted. But if she had been mistaken, if what she offered were not the things they indeed wanted, then her entire plan of action was in error.

While she claimed to want an intelligent, upstanding family man for a mate, she believed she could find him at the trendiest discos, bars and nightclubs. Whom she found there, of course, were the men who wanted from her what she was offering to give, to men who weren't there.

It didn't yet make sense to her.

"Vicki," I said, "I like you very much. I think you're terrific. But what you've been putting out is appropriate only as a playmate. You have to understand that, when men see you, they see only a good time, not the kind of emotional support and warmth you say you want to provide. You've never had a long-term relationship with a man, so you can't know what's missing. You have nothing to compare it to."

Vicki protested, claiming to know exactly what a man wants. As a man, I know she was correct in knowing what a man wants from a playmate.

"How do you distinguish," I asked her, "between someone you may want as a playmate and someone you want as a permanent mate?"

Again, her answer revealed that she knew only how to fulfill the role of a playmate.

"A permanent mate," I said, "is someone who is as involved in you as you are in him."

"Sure," she said, "I know that."

"But how involved are you in these men, Vicki? You know nothing at all about the kinds of work you want your man to do. What you are, Vicki, is a good time. 'For a good time, call Vicki.' That's the message you give off. But if they want to be nurtured, if they want to talk about their world, their emotions, their work, their problems, their joys, they're certainly not going to want to talk to you. You can't offer them anything, they think. What you've become, and therefore what you put out to the world, is party-time. You're fun, but that's all. At least, whatever depth of soul you have to offer doesn't show. You advertise shallowness, but when you get it you wonder why."

You may think that my lecture to Vicki was cruel. It wasn't. Rather than allow her to continue to bang her head against the mating wall, getting bloodied and bitter in the process, I wanted to show her that there was another way.

Vicki had to realize that, unless she drastically changed both her persona and her interests, she would not likely find her ideal man. She might, though, find an older man who was financially able to buy her the trappings she desired, someone who wanted merely companionship and a lively personality; or she might find a man whose intellectual orientation more closely matched her own.

Another Way

The understanding and the acceptance of these ideas came slowly and painfully to Vicki. After all, she had spent a lifetime developing her party-girl personality, and not developing any knowledge apart from where to shop and how to look prettier. She had never before considered that there may be a difference between a good date and a good mate, or that maybe people look for different things in mates and dates.

So it was to my surprise, and perhaps her own, when she opted for the more difficult choice. Rather than settle for someone less than she had wanted, she chose to change herself.

Between the newspaper and the library, she settled into the task: to become a more well-rounded personality, who could speak intelligently on, or at least seem interested in, a variety of topics.

You understand, I hope, that Vicki's decision was neither correct nor incorrect for the world at large. It makes no difference to me, and is no business of anyone else's, the kind of person anyone chooses to be or the mate he or she pursues.

Vicki embarked on an education reformation. Her desire was to understand what introspective people were like, so that she could make a comparison between her old lifestyle and one to which she'd never been exposed. This was an unusually powerful lifestyle decision.

To that end, she signed up for a three-day weekend with a group dedicated to contemplating geopolitical views. This experience exposed Vicki, for the first time in her life, to people whose lives didn't revolve constantly around money, clothes, fads, trends and sexual prowess.

Inspired by her adventure, she took a course at a local university in male-female relationships. Clearly, Vicki was on the road to becoming self-conscious.

To the best of my knowledge, Vicki still hasn't had a long-lasting relationship, but she has discovered herself. The last time we talked, she said she was more alone than she'd ever been in her life—"but not lonely." For the first time, she was enjoying being with herself, possibly because she knew herself for the first time. She stopped looking for validation elsewhere and started finding it inside herself.

She hadn't lost her sense of humor, however. "I think I'm a good catch," she said. "Too bad I can't subdivide. I'd like to have me over for dinner."

Discoveries

I found Vicki's transformation very exciting. Her journey was not easy for her, but it reveals once again that with determination and sweat we can change.

Vicki had to challenge years of media hype, social brain-washing, and a host of assumptions and beliefs. She had to be willing to take a hard look at herself through the eyes of others who did not have a vested interest in supporting her current beliefs. Vicki learned to punch her own ticket rather than seek validation from others.

During her journey, she discovered that healthy self-love is quite different than narcissistic love. She learned to love the inner self rather than merely the reflection in the mirror. She learned that she would often prefer her own company to that of the male bimbos and air-heads that populate the world looking for the Vicki of the past.

The Playboy
Aggressive, Assertive, Successful Ineffectiveness

When I first met Bill I was put off by him, just like every one else was. Bill is the male counterpart of Vicki. He covers his sensitive side with a bravado of self-assurance. He hides his feelings of inadequacy and insecurity with a facade of the most expensive goodies imaginable. He wears all the right jewelry and clothes, trying to catch the ladies who were always out of his reach. Even in high school Bill always wanted to catch the eye of one of the cheerleaders. He was always trying to impress someone in order to feel accepted.

Finally, Bill recognizes that something isn't working. He's not happy. He even feels uncomfortable when he does receive an invitation into the world which he so much admires. He simply feels out of place.

Then Bill discovers the very aspect of himself that he had been trying to hide in his strongest suit. He learns to look inside himself for meaning and to act on those feelings which give him the greatest satisfaction and joy. Bill turns himself inside out. As he begins to accept himself and make choices that surprise even him, Bill's life begins to change.

Bill

Bill, thirty-eight years old, was a good-looking, loud, aggressive rep for a line of women's clothing. His style of dress and the ostentatious manner in which he threw his money around identified him immediately as a "playboy."

Nevertheless, Bill said he was tired of playing the field and began searching for Miss Right. He wanted to meet an old-fashioned girl who would share his vision of nuptial bliss in a cottage surrounded by a white picket fence. Moreover, she was supposed to be his intellectual and physical equal.

Ball Busters or Angel Cakes

There was a huge dichotomy between what Bill said he wanted and what he really wanted. The women who were at least his intellectual and physical equal frightened him, and he called them "ball-busters". He'd try to go out with malleable women, only to get bored with them quickly, dismissing them as being too "mothering and demanding." Then he'd give autonomous, independent women another try, but because he could not dazzle them with his money, and their personalities were too challenging for his limited conception of women, he would switch back to the others, whom he called "Angel Cake."

Bill's money did not buy him class or style. Other men found him too competitive, while women thought he was overbearing. His sole hobby was to show off his latest trendy possession. He always wanted to fit in but felt like an outsider, even while hustling women in nightclubs and bars.

From a distance, Bill cut a terrific image, smart, strong, apparently sensitive, but as you got close to him he quickly became overbearing and boorish. He told everyone, and indeed may have thought, that he wanted an independent woman, but the fact is that when he found one, and she didn't conform to his rules, he quickly dropped her.

"I don't want someone who's going to cling to me," he proclaimed. "I get bored when they're like that. She's got to be very attractive, extremely attractive, gorgeous even. But she's also got to be financially and emotionally secure, educated and very sexual."

I asked him where he went to find someone like that. "Private clubs, trendy bars, places like that," he said.

"Have you found many women who fit the bill?" I asked.

"No." Pause. "Well, maybe a few."

"And what happened with them."

"I don't know. I guess we didn't see eye to eye."

What they didn't see eye to eye on, we later discovered together, was a definition of "independent." When these women wouldn't do, think and act the way Bill wanted, he grew frustrated and angry. And, of course, they did the same, finding themselves involved with a man who pretended to be one thing yet was another entirely.

The conflict extended even to sexual matters. Although Bill said he wanted someone aggressive and adventurous, he became impotent because he believed these were castrating females. The truth was, he was afraid of the women he said he wanted, while those that bored him were the only ones who would put up with his subterfuge. Actually, he both feared and admired the same woman and didn't know how to reconcile those conflicting feelings.

Bill was sincere about finding a solid relationship, but he wasn't serious about it. He couldn't have been. He had never truly examined the reality of what he wanted nor whether he himself possessed the qualities to which a person he believed he wanted would be attracted. He blamed women for his own inability to sustain a relationship.

Bill's mother had been overly indulgent and critical, and what he sought from a woman was nurturing. He could appreciate a woman's strength, as he did his mother's, but he wanted more tenderness and affection. He had always feared his mother's disapproval. Aggressive women made him feel inadequate by reminding him too much of her. Consequently, women to him were either too strong or too weak.

Bill's Big Three

In the self-inventory, Bill listed himself as aggressive, assertive and successful. To him, those were the Big Three.

His friends also attributed those same three characteristics to him, with the only difference being, they saw him as obnoxious, not appealing. The sword has two edges. Where he described himself as aggressive, they used the term hostile. They also added insensitive, boorish, intrusive and arrogant.

Bill described his ideal woman as strong-willed, independent, beautiful, wealthy, educated and very sexual.

Simply put, Bill thought he was hot Mirandas and any woman should be happy just to be seen with him. While the three adjectives he used to describe himself were accurate, he just didn't have any idea how true they were, how much of each he embodied. His whole personality style seemed to fit a single phrase: If a little of something is good, a lot is better.

"Excessive" was probably the word that described him best; he was just a little too much of everything.

Of course, being such a success in business because, he thought, of these characteristics, Bill was surprised by his friends' interpretation of him. The business world, with its immediate rewards, was the only point of reference Bill had. If they worked in business, the same tactics must be correct in all things.

He became defensive when confronted with his friends' views of him. He did not take too kindly to their feedback, despite having asked for their honesty. After soliciting their opinions, he spit the information back in their faces, as if they had intentionally tried to hurt him.

That he disputed their appraisal shouldn't have come as a shock, however, knowing that a certain dishonesty pervaded his entire personality. It was obvious to them, but not to him, that his desire for an independent and strong woman was just so much hot air, a desire to have a noble desire.

Bill's arguments with his friends about their reports only confirmed what he sought to dispel. Eventually, it became obvious even to him.

The self-inventory had revealed that, beneath all the glitz and bravado, Bill was frightened, shy and suffering from low self-esteem. Like all the other status symbols he wore, owned and drove, a modern woman would be just another piece of property Bill intended to add to his trendy collection. "I want a woman who's my equal," he said proudly, as if that statement indicated his enlightenment. What he wanted, in reality, was someone he could show off to his friends. If he had a Superwoman, that would mean, he believed, he was a Superman. He wanted the right woman, but for the wrong reasons. But what he discovered was that, unlike a Mercedes and a Rolex and a pair of Gucci loafers, independent women have minds of their own. And therein lay the conflict.

Interestingly, Bill's subconscious probably knew instinctively what his conscious mind didn't: that intelligent and independent women would see right through his veneer. So rather than seek his so-called ideal mate in places she might be found, he haunted the kinds of places where his tinsel was respected and even worshipped. And when, by chance, he occasionally got close to the kind of woman he said he wanted, he would instantly degrade her verbally. This was certainly preferable, he knew, to being pegged as an inadequate little nerd, which was how he felt inside.

I told Bill that he had three options if he still wanted to find a permanent mate: One, he could examine how his antagonistic and abrasive behavior was offensive to a sensitive woman, and work to change it. Two, he could recognize this aspect of himself and accept the reality that, being who he was, only with more docile, subservient women would he stand a chance of maintaining a permanent relationship. Or three, with some introspection, and using the self-inventory as a starting point, he could work to increase his self-esteem by emphasizing his strengths rather than over-compensating for his weaknesses. That way, he might find the right women available to him.

Bill's Tender Side

While he doubted how clear cut his alternatives were, the self-inventory was clearly working, at least, on an unconscious level. When he attended parties at which other loud, boorish men were loud and boorish, the kinds of events he always felt most comfortable at, Bill was able to recognize that he had the same characteristics. He saw how unattractive and unappealing they were. He began not to feel all that comfortable in these environments, buying a few too many drinks for too many people he didn't know, trying a little too hard to make contact.

Slowly, almost imperceptibly, the changes occurred in Bill. And one night, he found himself sitting in a bar feeling like an outsider. Everything was too fast, furious, loud and raunchy, too laden with sexual innuendo.

So he kept trying different bars. Eventually, he found that he felt most comfortable with so-called blue-collar types, working people. They weren't necessarily poor, but there was an earthiness about them he found appealing. He could strike up conversations without feeling either overeducated or undereducated, without feeling that he had to impress anyone with the make of his car, the size of his house, or the karats in his diamond pinkie ring. These people, he said to me one day, seemed "real" to him.

At this one particular bar he frequented there were always games of darts and backgammon being played, and to his surprise, Bill was good at both of them. So good, in fact, that he became known for his skill, which enhanced his self-esteem. For perhaps the first time in his life, he felt comfortable in social situations.

Bill also did something very unusual: he became a Big Brother to a twelve-year-old boy whose father had died several years before. This experience brought out another side of him, the more tender side, and showed him that he liked the responsibility of caring, without tangible rewards, for another human.

The boy looked up to Bill, which was actually the greatest reward Bill ever received. A peripheral reward came when he would talk about his "little brother" to women. They loved his sensitivity, and for that, he got the kinds of rewards he had previously thought were available to him only when he pushed.

A few years down the line, Bill married an "earth woman" who had two children, a teenage son and a pre-teen daughter, from a previous marriage. Placed in the role of provider, and not worrying whether he was impressing everyone, he found himself on comfortable ground. His step-children grew to adore him, and the feelings were, the last time I heard, mutual. Rather than bragging about his jewelry, his car, or his bank account, he pulled out his family photographs and showed them off proudly.

Finally, Bill had been accepted into a group. And he had an identity: husband and father.

Discoveries

Bill's story demonstrates how we can hide our best personality characteristics even from ourselves. It shows how attempts at covering our true self can lead to a life of dissatisfaction and unhappiness. Often our world teaches us that there is only one way to achieve happiness. It teaches us that glitz and dazzle are the keys to a life of fulfillment.

Bill took that route and found that it led to nowhere. He felt deceived. He then had to go back to the fork in the road and choose another way. This route was less familiar and less popular. His journey turned inward, and for Bill this was quite a shift. Bill had placed everything on the outside. He was the consummate materialist believing that happiness and meaning could be bought.

By looking inward, he found another set of values that regarded people above things; people rather than looks; and real people over celebrities and titles.

Cruising the Fast Lane
She Scared the Men She Wanted Most

Linda was the type of woman that Bill would have sought out. And had they met there would have been a loud crash as their facades and egos collided. Beneath her brash exterior we will discover a warm, loving human being who wanted a loving relationship.

However, Linda also wanted to continue in her very successful business that she had started from scratch. She felt that she was caught between her desire to maintain a single life, have an affectionate relationship, and her cultural imperative which stated that she should be married and have children. She had developed a lifestyle that preserved her autonomy, allowed her to have male contact, and gave her an excuse for not finding a husband: "there aren't any decent men out there." However, she felt like a fraud.

Through her journey, Linda makes peace with herself. Pay attention to how she is able to accept herself and her own desires. Note the discrepancies between what she says and what she does, and how she reconciles her inner desires for autonomy with her need for connectedness and affection.

Linda

Linda, forty-two, held her own extremely well in the business world, and she, too, flitted from man to man, never sustaining a relationship longer than a month. She lived in the fast lane, where she was comfortable cruising at high speeds. She was on a first name basis with every bartender in town. Observing her, you would have thought she preferred to remain single, yet she complained bitterly about her inability to meet the right man.

If the cruel truth be known, Linda was a little too loud, a little too bawdy, a little too everything for what she said she wanted. While she believed that she was sophisticated and psychologically aware, she really had very little insight into her behavior. She attributed the world's inability to deal with her overtly sexual stance and aggressive behavior to it being "their problem." "If they can't deal with my directness," she'd say, "screw 'em."

The Contradictions

Beneath the bravado, Linda was warm, sensitive and good-hearted. She was easily hurt by men and felt awful when rejected. And she truly had no clue why.

Although Linda had many friends, the closest being other females or gay men, none were very intimate.

Linda was full of contradictions. "I want to have a relationship," she proclaimed. "I want to get married."

"What kind of man are you looking for?" I asked her.

"A sensitive, caring man," she said, "who's willing to make a commitment, but not be too possessive. It's important to me to continue my career, and I travel a lot, so I want a man who's going to be able to pick up and go with me at a moment's notice. And he has to be fun-loving."

I was impressed by the clarity of her vision, even if skeptical about such a man's existence. Who, after all would be willing to submerge his own identity at the whim of his partner, except a man who lacked the type of strong will she said she wanted? I asked her where she goes to find such a man.

"Cocktail lounges," she said. "And sometimes parties."

I asked her what kind of man she usually dates. "Unfortunately," she said, "they turn out to be married. I don't understand why, but it seems like every guy I end up going out with is cheating on his wife."

It wasn't difficult to see that Linda was scaring away the very men she said she wanted. Whenever a man got close to her, her sensitive and caring side was supplanted by her purely sexual self. Naturally, the vast majority of men attracted to her on any given night were players, men fooling around, either on their wives or just for the fun of it. The sensitive and committed men Linda claimed to seek had probably run far for cover.

Conversely, the men who responded to Linda were actually responding appropriately to the type of message she transmitted: that she was looking to play, not get involved seriously. To help her to align her intentions with her actions, we relied heavily on the self-inventory.

In her self-inventory, Linda listed herself as sensitive, charming, funny, gutsy, loyal, generous, cute, independent, bright and competent.

Interestingly, her friends viewed her very much the same, except that they felt she was often more crass, emotionally volatile, headstrong and demanding; and sometimes, they believed, she was unreasonable, obstinate and recalcitrant.

Linda's version of her ideal mate described him as warm, sensitive, caring, intelligent, fun, committed, sexual, flexible, flexible and flexible.

It was one of Linda's friends who noted that, although Linda's characteristics generally matched her ideal mate's, her emphasis on flexibility and her own obstinacy would probably make any permanent relationship difficult.

When she reported that back to me, claiming to be misunderstood, I told her that I thought her friend was absolutely correct. At forty-two, Linda had lived alone for so long she was used to doing things her way and her way only. With the exception of her brief and stormy marriage, she had not been able to live with a man for more than a weekend without wanting either one of them to be somewhere else. The word compromise was not in her lexicon.

Changing the Fantasy

When I suggested to Linda that all of the data seemed to indicate that she was not a particularly good candidate to be a wife, she got angry. Everything about her, her single-minded career goals and aspirations, all of what made her the charming person she was, skewed away from a permanent relationship. Her personality was not congruent with what it takes to achieve permanence and stability.

Linda's attitudes about marriage had been formed for her by a culture which says that permanence and stability, i.e. marriage, are the ultimate goals for a normal person. She had internalized, or tried to internalize, those values, given to her by her parents, her grandparents, her aunts and uncles, but she could not conform to the model.

Rather than admit that permanence wasn't for her, Linda preferred a complete and total personality metamorphosis, contorting to fit what she said she wanted. She tried to fulfill what she thought she should be doing, or what others wanted her to do. Instead of changing her fantasy to fit her individuality, her nature and temperament, she tried to squeeze herself through the keyhole of some predetermined concept of normality.

Linda's romantic past was littered with the psychic corpses of men who conformed perfectly to what she said she wanted but couldn't satisfy what she needed: a fun-loving male who would be there when Linda wanted and absent when she didn't, who would be willing to play second fiddle to her career and be understanding of her independent nature. Aside from a Casper Milquetoast, who would never have been able to satisfy her anyway because of his lifeless personality, only a series of playmates fit Linda's needs, the very men she had been dating and dropping because they didn't correspond to what she said she wanted.

The question for Linda became, would she continue her doomed pursuit of a committed relationship, or realize that ordinary marriage is not necessarily for everyone?

"Linda," I asked her, "how many men do you really think are willing to stop their career at a moment's notice to satisfy your whims?"

"Not many," she admitted.

"And if they're not willing to become subservient to you, are you willing to become subservient to their whims?"

"Certainly not," she said.

"Well, your words say one thing, but your actions speak differently. What your really want is a playmate, not a permanent mate."

Although the statement was first met with denial, Linda objectively examined the evidence of her own behavior. The poignant truth became clear: she was trying to please those in her family who felt she ought to perform her biological functions. While she was perfectly comfortable in the single life she had developed for herself, which really didn't have room for a man on a permanent basis, the gnawing sense of guilt she felt for not fulfilling her parents' wishes was strong enough to induce a grand charade.

When Linda acknowledged that she did not really want to maintain a permanent relationship, she breathed a sigh of relief that expelled thirty-odd years of hypocrisy, and she cried.

For Linda, and people like her who cannot, or do not want to, abide by the constrictions inherent in a permanent one-on-one relationship, a succession of specialized playmates is a perfectly acceptable alternative. Linda had tossed away many men in the past because they hadn't satisfied her apparent desire for a jack-of-all-trades. Yet these very men were wonderful playmates who, had she known then what she learned through the self-inventory, would have made perfect additions to a stable of dates designed to satisfy particular needs or moods.

Once she chose to accept her preference for being a single woman, she was able to move on with her life. She used the program, literally, to improve the quality of the playmates she chose. Whereas before she avoided obvious singles hangouts, like bars and clubs, because those places probably would not have yielded the type of permanent mate she thought she was looking for, she now focused on going to milieus where specific specialized playmates could be found.

An Affirmation

Knowing now that she was searching for a series of playmates, each fitting a different desire and purpose in her life, Linda decided to take an affirmative stance by placing an ad in one of the more prestigious local magazines. Doing so was, in essence, her public statement, aimed primarily at her family: she was now going to assume control over her life.

The ad read: "Wanted: fun-loving, unattached man, fortyish-fiftyish, sometimes sophisticated, sometimes not; no cohabitation, but not opposed to having a long-term companion to attend events like the Philharmonic opening, ballet, concerts, etc. I am an independent, educated, professional woman—cute, vivacious, outgoing and aggressive—who likes travel and adventure (*la dolce vita*), but doesn't want to be caged."

After making this public declaration, Linda had to go around and change all of her friends' and colleagues' beliefs about her, that she was in the market for a particular type of permanent mate. They were skeptical at first, accusing her simply of copping out because of the troubles she had finding Mr. Right. But between the ad (which yielded several good possibilities), and defending her right to be single, the concept took comfortable root in her mind and soul. She found herself feeling freer to tell her professional acquaintances as well.

Just as a fun experiment, Linda also joined a dating service and met a couple of men, neither of whom appealed much to her. She also joined riding and tennis clubs, which were two of her passions.

Linda became extraordinarily successful in her business, enjoying it much more than she had while looking for, she thought, a permanent mate. The hours she used to fret over having to find a husband, she put into her work. According to her friends, once she became accepting of her career dedication, her outspokenness lost much of its desperate edge. They said that she was much easier to be around, and they even liked her choice of playmates.

Linda's mother, she reported with smile, never got comfortable with her decision to remain single. "I'm forty-four years-old," Linda said, "and she thinks it's a phase I'm going through."

Discoveries

Linda's struggle is not unique. Many women of her age are confronted with the question: "So how come you're not married?" It gets old for all of them. The typical response is some version of "all the good men are either married or gay." Even in this time of enlightenment, men and women, but especially women, are looked upon with a raised eyebrow when they are still single at forty. They are often made to feel guilty and embarrassed having to make excuses for themselves and wondering what is wrong with them.

In order to deal with the issue, they find ways to appease their family and friends as well as the part of themselves that has internalized the cultural imperative "thou shall marry." They seem to seek inappropriate mates. In this way they can appear as though they are mate-shopping, while preserving their single status. However, this approach is tiring; it takes a lot of energy to continue the charade.

Linda decided to proclaim herself "single by choice." Eventually her friends, and even her family, accepted this.

The "Widow Smith"
Rebuilding Romance

Margaret is a woman in mourning. She is grieving the loss of her husband of thirty years. She feels guilty when she thinks of other men, and depressed about her loss and her life. She tries to make do and accept her plight, but also harbors resentment for believing that, at fifty-five, her life is over. The last time Margaret dated anyone was back in the 1950s. She had no concept of dating in the 1990s.

So Margaret had to go through a metamorphoses, changing from a 1950-60s housewife with traditional values, hiding behind her role as wife and mother, and enter the world of the nineties. In some respects it was as jarring for Margaret as leaving an air-conditioned movie theater on a hot summer's day.

Margaret

Margaret, fifty-five, had been widowed about two years prior to seeing me for the first time. A housewife for all of her thirty-year marriage, she found herself ill-prepared for the modern dating game, the world having changed a great deal since she and her husband socialized with the other kids at the malt shop.

Margaret grew up in a small town with small town values. Her husband was the boy-next-door, and their life together could have been mistaken for Ozzie and Harriet.

Raising children and caring for her husband was her career, and his sudden stroke, short illness and subsequent death left her sad, confused and angry. While she was not destitute, neither did their assets guarantee lifetime security for her. Thrown into both the job and man markets at the same time, she had to face the fact that she could no longer get by solely on her looks.

After a long mourning period, Margaret tried to put her life back together, a life, she knew, that would have to be very different from her married one. When she realized it was time to begin dating, she went into therapy. Why she did is easy to figure out. The last time she'd dated was in college, and that was the boy who became her husband. A typical date then consisted of dinner and maybe a movie. She was a virgin when she married, and the thought of getting romantically involved in this era of sexual freedom and women's rights terrified her.

Dropping the "Mrs." Facade

Still attractive, if a bit overweight, Margaret seemed shy; she had always hidden behind the "Mrs." facade, and now she was confronted with rebuilding and recreating. She knew she would have to change much of what she had previously thought, including her attitudes towards sex: it had been something she enjoyed, but not too often, and then mostly for the benefit of her husband. After all, a woman's role, she thought, was to please her husband, and "men need sex more than women."

Her first exposure to men on any sort of a romantic level was through friends, specifically, the husbands of her friends, who were coming on to her, flirting with her behind their wives' backs. Not surprisingly, those situations evoked mixed feelings in her. Although she felt the advances were improper, she also found herself strangely turned on and invigorated. It reminded her of her youth, when she had been lovely enough to attract many boys.

During our first sessions together, Margaret had to deal with her guilt over seeing other men. I facilitated that process, I think, by getting her to itemize honestly the qualities she thought she wanted now in a mate. When I asked her what type of man she was looking for, she fairly described her husband, which was no surprise considering he had been the only man she ever had known intimately.

What Became of Jim? Occasionally during her married life, Margaret admitted, she allowed her imagination to ruminate on "Jim," the other young man who had competed directly against her husband for her affections. What had become of him, she wondered? While certainly more vibrant and exciting than her husband, Jim had had no concrete plans for the future, as had her husband. He could promise her only vague uncertainties, whereas her husband's sensible plan provided her with assurances. The daughter of a Depression-era couple who emphasized financial stability over all other things, including romance, Margaret opted for safety. It was only on rainy and gloomy afternoons, when she felt kind of down anyway, that she regretted her choice. She did love her husband, though.

Now, circumstances were different. Although her husband hadn't, by any means, left her independently wealthy, Margaret's need for the type of security her husband provided wasn't as great as her desire for some sort of adventure, that which she had missed out on by marrying him. In the 1950s, the period in which she and her husband met and married, sexual adventure was considered taboo, and, being a good girl, she strictly observed the tradition of the times. During their marriage, they had sex infrequently, and then only at his urging. While she enjoyed it, she did "it," she thought, for his benefit.

After she told me about Jim, I read back to her the characteristics she had given me of the type of man she wanted: loyal, responsible, steady, secure, a good provider, intelligent, calm and understanding. She hesitated before finally whispering, "Boring."

Of course, admitting that induced in her some gut-wrenching guilt. She cried and begged God to forgive her for what she felt was a sacrilege, a pox on her husband's soul.

In time, Margaret came to realize that life was for the living, and that wanting to move on with her life and participate in it did not make her an evil person.

Now, Margaret tentatively admitted, she wanted to meet someone who would turn her on. Someone like Ricardo Montalban, she said sheepishly, as though she were playing a game, as though someone else were speaking the words. She didn't necessarily want to settle down; she wanted to have fun, she added, laughing uncomfortably at her own admission.

The widower dentist with whom she was fixed up about fourteen months after her husband died had been, she said, a "very nice man," but she wasn't turned on by him, nor by his money. The same was true of every other man she met through the church group in which she and her husband had been very active and around which most of their friends were centered. She concluded that, by staying in the same social sphere as she had been when her husband was alive, she would continue to meet only the same kind of men as he.

Going Through the Motions

Uncharacteristically brazen, she decided to stretch—sort of.

In search of "Ricardo Montalban," Margaret widened her social arena to include the kinds of activities in which she imagined him to be interested: the theater, university extension courses, a myriad of cultural events. I applauded her efforts, noting that she was apparently fitting her sampling technique to her stated aim.

Well, she proclaimed the efforts a failure after about six weeks. "It didn't work," she told me.

I asked whether she belonged to a theatre group or went alone. "Alone," she answered. The same was true of the other events she attended.

I asked about the types of seminars or classes she enrolled in. Each of them had to do with so-called women's issues: women in business, the changing role of the American woman, etc.

Quite simply, Margaret's actions spoke louder and much more clearly than her tentative admissions about wanting a different kind of mate. She was only going through the motions of proper sampling. She did not really want her efforts to result in success.

Like many people, Margaret's ambivalence demonstrated her unconscious resistance to the idea of systematically developing a strategy of finding a mate. She did all the right things in all the wrong ways.

When we got to the self-inventory, Margaret was able to examine both her modus operandi and her motives. She rated herself as: rather plain, plain looking, somewhat boring, not too bright, not much to offer, competent only in menial things, a good mother, a loyal friend and a fair cook. Hardly a glowing report card from someone, I felt, who had so much to offer.

Her friends rated her much differently: attractive, bright (but not informed) capable and warm.

Margaret's dream lover embodied just about everything she thought she wasn't: attractive, witty, debonair, sexual, a good dresser, sophisticated, adventurous, even slightly dangerous.

Over the years, Margaret, a former homecoming queen, had necessarily had to substitute the sparkle and zest of her youth with maternal and wifely worries. Having married less for love (although certainly that, too) than security, she had since lost the devilish charm that was her trademark as a girl. She felt now that the future held little promise——she was resigned——while a past she had not lived was gone.

Despite that pessimism, Margaret needed only to realize that the blanket of dowdiness she had come to wear everyday was entirely disposable, and that her friends view of her was much more correct than her own. In other words, her dream mate could, with a little tweaking, be well within her grasp.

Exploring the Possible

The first attitude to explore was the one she held of herself as the eternal wife/mother. With her husband having passed on, and her children grown and living their own lives, Margaret still could not dispel the self-image she had maintained for thirty years. Even though there were no more wifely/motherly duties, she clung to the familiar facade for security.The truth, I thought and told her, was that she no longer felt sexual.

"I used to be pretty, but no more," she lamented. What man, she wondered, would ever be attracted to "this old face and body." The fact that neither her body nor her face looked her age was irrelevant, because she felt old, fat and ugly. Fortunately, her friends' appraisal caused her to reconsider. One friend had written: "Like a fine piece of marble, Margaret has all the potential to be sculpted into great art. All she needs are the hands."

Margaret, flattered, took that statement in two ways: one, she ought to improve her face and body with the help of professionals, makeup and exercise people; and two, she ought to "get laid." She admitted that reluctantly when I asked her what she thought her friend's words had meant.

The first interpretation she was willing to try, because she had nothing to lose. But the second, having an affair, was much more difficult for her. Margaret felt that, while physically she may have still had the "potential," emotionally and mentally she had nothing to offer the type of man she wanted. "What's the point?" she said. "It would be a disaster. Why should I bother?"

"What have you ever failed at in your life?" I asked her.

She was silent, thinking, probably, of a life she never lived—not that she necessarily regretted her choice, but now the past seemed so much more romantic. Where once there had been curiosity, now there was only denial.

I repeated the question.

"I guess nothing," she said.

"Then what makes you think you have nothing to offer?"

Again, she was silent. Eventually, I persuaded her to see that everything she had ever tried to do she had done better than average. But, having opted for security rather than adventure, she had always sensed a sort of unconscious gnawing: What Might Have Been. And she therefore felt her pleasant, uneventful family life had been a failure.

Because she had performed her tasks so well, raising a family and keeping a house, Margaret downplayed her accomplishments. In fact, anyone who has ever tried to raise a family and keep a house knows how difficult those tasks are to do well.

While she was resistant to working through her feelings of incompetence and inadequacy, it was even more difficult to convince her that her reawakened sexual longings were normal and healthy.

She admitted in whispered tones, her knees locked together, that she had found herself strangely turned on by the grocery clerk, as well as some of her friends' sons.

Having those feelings, and acting on them, are entirely different, I told her. Nevertheless, there was no reason why she shouldn't pursue a sexual adventure with an appropriate mate. Which brought us back to her dream lover.

Again, she said, a man like him wouldn't want a woman like her.

Suffice it to say that, eventually, Margaret decided to go in for a complete make over: physical and mental. After joining a gym and exercising away some of the accumulated years, she bought a new and decidedly unmatronly wardrobe in which to show off her new figure. Then she got a job, part-time, in a school, which instantly helped improve her self-esteem; she was making things happen. She also took some college extension courses in subjects she had always wanted to learn.

The result stemming from her self-inventory and introspection: a new Margaret who no longer felt unworthy of "Ricardo Montalban." All that was left for her was to find him.

To do that, Margaret expanded her rather traditional list of agents, her girlfriends, to include her beautician, who seemed to have a direct pipeline to all the eligible singles in town. She also joined a dating service, both to meet new men and to see how new men responded to her. Reflecting her caution, Margaret drove thirty-five miles out of town to the service, as much for the company's reputation as for the guarantee that, thirty-five miles away, she wouldn't run across any of the single men she already knew.

Margaret told me afterward that the process of being interviewed there helped solidify the self-inventory experience for her. Answering similar questions allowed her to reexamine the conclusions she had reached on her own.

While the dating service became her primary agent, and yielded four good leads, Margaret also ventured out on her own. She joined a another gym which had a juice and snack bar so that she wouldn't always have to work out to be in view. It allowed her to see how other people, including those younger than herself, interacted.

Between the men she met through her friends, her beautician and the dating service, and the knowledge (if not men) gained through the health club, she was able finally to experience how men related to her as just Margaret, not "the widow Smith."

Eventually, Margaret discovered that she must have been a big-city girl in another life. After moving to New York, she opened a small travel agency. The last I heard of her, she was on a cruise—ostensibly, she said, to investigate accommodations—in the Mediterranean. She had, she told me, been dating a "very, very interesting" man, one among many.

Discoveries

Margaret realized that life doesn't end with the death of a mate. Through self-exploration and experimentation, she discovered her own vitality. She confronted her feelings of inadequacy and through her personal inventory began to nurture her skills and expand her interests, gradually achieving a sense of competence and mastery.

Too often people bite off more than they can chew, leading themselves to failure and discouragement. When we are changing, we must take baby-steps in order to avoid overwhelming ourselves. It is dangerous to assume that you "should" be able to take bigger bites. Success and self-confidence, like a pearl necklace, is built by stringing one pearl at a time.

Margaret didn't try to change her life all at once. It was a series of slow steps, sometimes two forward and one back; and sometimes two forward and three back. Change occurs gradually. Like in Margaret's case, we often have many years of habit and history affecting our choices. We rarely stop to explore these beliefs unless confronted by a crisis. However, we do not have to wait for a crisis. We can start now.

The Mama's Boy
Searching for a Dream Girl

Robert is the prototype of the compulsive, overachieving, perfectionistic young man for whom competence, performance, and intellectual pursuits were the *sine qua non* of being a good boy. He sacrificed his leisure time and most of his adolescence. When other boys were learning how to relate to girls, to each other, and to their bodies, Robert spent his time studying, fantasizing, and listening to sports on television or radio. Thus, like Donna, when it comes to interpersonal relationships, Robert is still sixteen.

He sees women as sexual objects and himself as a nerd. He has become a caricature of the 1990s man; when he gets dressed he looks like he is wearing the look of success without the feeling of success.

Robert's journey leads him to discover his own values appropriate to a thirty-six-year-old adult and, at the same time, gives him the opportunity to let the inner child have some fun. He has to learn that he is not the nerd he might have thought himself to be as a youth. He has to discover that thirty-six-year-olds can enjoy life without being caught in a time warp.

In order to grow, and to integrate his inner child with his accomplished adult, he must finally leave home; he must, metaphorically, leave his mother.

Robert

Robert was thirty-six. He lived at home until he got his first engineering job at age twenty-five after finishing graduate school. Extraordinarily bright, capable, well-respected, reliable, responsible, were the attributes everyone else saw in him. Inside, he felt self-conscious and guilt-ridden. He believed he was only as good as his last job performance and that he had no other value as a human being other than his "performances."

In some senses, Robert was the classic mama's boy. He and his controlling mother maintained a close relationship, and she was the supreme arbiter of right and wrong, good and bad. Never mind that her experience with dating was confined solely to Robert's father. She gave the impression (and Robert believed) that she had all the answers about dating. Robert never questioned her or her credentials.

Robert's father was a Milquetoast who limited his parenting to bringing home the bacon. If pressed, Robert could barely guess his father's opinion on a number of subjects. His major contribution to Robert's view of romance was to provide a role-model: give women what they want and then withdraw.

Dream Girl

When Robert conjured up his "dream girl," he pictured a Playboy Playmate who also possessed intelligence, wit and charm—as though such a woman would want anything to do with him. His major fantasies were to answer the door in a towel after a shower to find the Avon girl waiting to be seduced, and entering the wrong room in a hotel to find a gorgeous woman spreading her legs at the sight of him.

While he spent a few nights a week at a bar, chains around his neck, smiling self-consciously at girls (never women!), he almost always went home alone to his stamp collection. Most of his dates were with the college-student daughters of his mother's friends, who were just as withdrawn. He trembled with nervousness in the presence of females to whom he was attracted, putting them on a pedestal, believing them to be perfect. But, if one of them should like him in spite of himself, he instantly questioned whether something was wrong with her; after all, as Groucho Marx said, "I wouldn't want to belong to a club that would have me as a member."

Robert believed that the Playboy Playmate who graced his mailbox each month was perfect. These women, whether pictured in the pages of men's magazines or the reasonable facsimiles thereof he saw walking down the street, seemed to be the epitome of success to Robert.

Of course, his concept of success was completely one-dimensional. He believed simply that these perfect women would be the perfect complement to the perfect engineer. He imagined himself making perfect love and having perfect conversations with this woman; in his mind, they were perfectly compatible.

In reality, Robert's fantasies were not about women with whom he had anything in common, nothing that would engender any sort of long-term relationship, but about a playmate whose physical beauty would, he felt, satisfy his every need.

And why not? What kind of person, after all, could be more distant from his mother, the one who over-protected and over-sheltered him, than a Playboy Playmate, who represents sex and danger?

As a child, Robert led (not uncoincidentally) a one-dimensional life. The focus was on using his considerable brain power. Consequently, he developed into a socially inept, awkward adolescent and adult with no social skills whatsoever. Only his passion for sports enabled him to interact successfully with others outside his work. By the time he found himself interested in mating, he hadn't tasted enough foods, so to speak, to develop a knowledgeable palate. He had absolutely no criteria for knowing what he truly wanted in a woman, so he projected onto beautiful, sexy women all the attributes he found appealing.

Interestingly, on meeting Robert, one would not likely suspect that his fantasies were so blatantly dichotomous from the "good boy" image his mother had shaped. A respected professional who dated all the "nice girls" his mother set him up with, he felt, with burning intensity, the burden of having to be the sort of good husband and father his family expected of him. Yet the women who would have qualified to fill the role, giving him a safe home and children, bored him.

Robert knew that having a Playboy Playmate as a wife was an unrealistic expectation for him. Not because such a woman apparently wouldn't fit into the mold he had to fill, but because he felt that she was unattainable. He believed that he was too much of a nebbish to ever get her. And he was right.

So, after dating these nice, plain girls whom he wasn't particularly attracted to, he often "made love" to hookers, pretending they were his dream girl. Hookers, he knew, would not reject him. They were the only women with whom he had ever had sex.

On the most fundamental level, Robert felt that he had missed out on the sexual revolution, and he wanted to make up for lost time. He wanted to go back to his youth. But, as the sexual revolution had passed him by, so too had the maturation process, which was the more essential missing ingredient keeping him from participating in the present. He was caught in an unending cycle of embarrassment, at his own social and sexual shortcomings, and fear of admitting that his shortcomings existed. As a perfectionist, which was precisely the driven quality that made him such a profound success in his profession, he could not allow the type of woman he considered to be perfect to discover that his performance would be less than that. Hookers, he knew, wouldn't feel let down by his inability to match the expectations he hoped for himself as a lover. But hookers couldn't help him socially, so he remained stuck in a quagmire of his own creation.

As one who, at age thirty-six, had achieved great success in his chosen profession, and earned and deserved respect, Robert approached women as the same, inept eighteen year-old college sophomore who was unable to look a girl in the eye.

In accordance with his desire to redo the past, Robert hung out wherever college students and playmate types congregated, places like college bars, discos and private clubs. So far, so good—his was an approach beyond reproach to finding his targeted woman. He was an outsider, a kind of pathetic fringe player trying to wear the right clothes and jewelry and say the hip things. The irony is that, in his youth, he had been so unsophisticated socially that the mere thought of contact with a woman broke him out in hives, and he had avoided social scenes. Now, his professional successes had bolstered his confidence just enough to make himself seem foolish. After establishing contact, he had nothing else to say. He lacked the ability to engage in the kind of small talk necessary for these women, who were willing to forgive many of his shortcomings because of his obvious affluence, which he wore ostentatiously on his fingers, around his neck, on his feet and in the type of car he drove.

Forever Out of Reach

So here was this successful professional who had spent the first thirty-five years of his life being serious, being, in his mother's words of encouragement, "a little man," trying earnestly to make serious contact with girls half his age while acting half his. A more potent formula for failure, you would be hard-pressed to find. He was faced with the fact that the equation didn't compute. But instead of using his formidable grey matter to figure out that the components could never equal out, he would blame himself. "There's something wrong with me," he would say. "I can't connect with them."

Robert made great progress, though, in the self-inventory. He wrote down: withdrawn, scared, unattractive and socially inept.

By contrast, his friends, all male, described him as bright, average to better-than-average looking, mildly athletic, witty, funny, a good observer, practical and knowledgeable about almost all things.

As we already know, the characteristics Robert attributed to his ideal mate were: beautiful, sexy, intelligent and a good conversationalist.

Obviously, Robert's self-image was so poor that the woman of his dreams seemed infinitely distant from his ability ever to meet and mate with her. So you can imagine his surprise when he discovered what his friends had to say about him.

In trying to understand the disparity between his self-image and the one his friends had of him, Robert told me that nothing he ever did as a kid was good enough for his parents. He may have scored 98 on a test in school, but his parents were only concerned with the two points he missed. Their constant berating of him caused him to underrate his undeniable academic success, believing it was due only to his excellent memory, not intelligence.

Having skipped ahead a couple of grades in school, Robert was always younger than the other kids in his classes. So, in already operating from the point of view that he would be criticized unless he was perfect, and wanting and needing to prove himself to his older classmates, Robert felt he had to be better than them—hence, the origins of his perfectionism.

He believed that if he could have the best girlfriend, then he'd be accepted by his classmates; if he could attain good enough, then he'd be a success. But since nothing he ever did was good enough, "best" and "good enough," by definition, would be forever out of his reach.

Not surprisingly, these attitudes carried over into adulthood, where they grew more obfuscated and complex. His entire world became centered around these hopelessly unobtainable concepts. Whatever came easily to him, no matter how difficult it may have been for others, he devalued and belittled. He trivialized his accomplishments and emphasized his inabilities. No matter how many achievements, completions or successes he might experience, a single disappointment or so-called failure brought him to the brink of disaster; he was only as good as his last "performance."

Those feelings of inadequacy were confirmed repeatedly by his difficulties with women. Being so much more cerebral than the women he sought, and anyway lacking such basic social abilities as chit-chat, Robert could not easily move past the "hello-how-are-you?" stage. Whenever he went on a date with a woman who had any of the qualities on his most-desired list, the attitude implicit in his voice was, "You don't want to be with me, do you?" Of course, considering the tone, the answer was usually no. And if, by chance, a woman did want to be with him, she immediately became suspect. The more unattainable they were, the more allure they held for him. If they liked him, he thought, how good could they really be?

Rather than pursuing women for the joy and pleasure of the relationships which might develop, Robert found that he wanted women in order to gain acceptance, as if showing off to the world a trophy clutching his arm.

Becoming His Own Agent

Seeing himself for the first time through more objective eyes, the eyes of people who knew him well, Robert realized that he had been pretending for most of his life. The truth, he learned via the self-inventory, was that he had long since been twenty-two years old, and that trying to turn back the clock and relive the sexual revolution which had passed him by was impossible. He learned that his inability to consummate sexually with the women he had held in such high-esteem meant that he needed something more intimate than wham-bam-thank-you-maam, and that before wham and after bam, he wanted more than thank you.

He learned that being seen with, or even having sex with, a gorgeous body wouldn't necessarily earn him the respect and acceptance he had wanted; those could come only from himself. He once told me that, having finally made love to a gorgeous woman, he couldn't wait, after climaxing, to get up and call all his friends, as if the experience wouldn't be complete without their knowledge and approval. I told him about the man who was asked by his friend whether he'd had a good time on his European vacation. "I don't know," the man replied. "I haven't had my pictures developed yet." And anyway, his friends had already thought of him the way he had wanted to be thought of.

That particular realization represented the biggest surprise.

At thirty-six, Robert began to accept himself, warts and all. When that happened, he was free to pursue a two-pronged program: first, to meet the playmates of his dreams for whatever recreational or entertainment purposes might occur; and second, to find an appropriate permanent mate.

No longer did Robert subscribe to the all-or-none principle. Now that he could distinguish between the two, he found both tasks much easier.

In essence, Robert became his own agent by making himself more accessible at work. Rather than becoming invisible or remaining chained behind his desk each time there was an office function, he began to socialize with his co-workers. Soon, he even left work early a few times with some of them, both male and female, to have a few beers at a bar and watch sporting events on the establishment's TV.

When he came to believe that his colleagues no longer thought of him as a nerd, he felt able to venture out alone to the same bars, where many of the other regulars had already gotten to know him. "Hi, Rob," or "Hi, Bob," the other regulars called out to him. And soon he was capable of braving unknown waters, going into bars and lounges where he didn't know anyone else, experimenting with different kinds of dress, depending on the mood he was in.

On Robert's initiative, the company organized a co-ed softball team, and he was made captain. The team joined a league and each week played a game, after which there was always a bit of a party attended by both sides.

These days, Robert is that tall, kind of good-looking man you see at the bar, the one who always seems to know everyone and carry on long-winded conversations about who-knows-what. You know him as "that friendly guy over there."

He's still single, playing the field, as it were. He likes all the women he goes out with, and they like him. But he's not ready to make anything permanent, not yet. After all, he said, it hasn't been that long since his palms got all sweaty in any female's presence.

Discoveries

Robert's story emphasizes the importance of maintaining a balanced life, mixing both achievement and mastery, on the one hand, and pleasure and fun on the other. Too many folks believe that they can put all of their energy into the pursuit of financial success and then, once achieved, they can easily turn to the world of play.

Robert lived primarily in a fantasy world when it came to interpersonal relations, especially with women. The two sets of values he internalized were in conflict; one was represented by his mother who preached delay of gratification, and the other, represented by *Playboy*, exalted immediate, material, and sexual gratification. While the system promoted by his mother taught him restraint and the value of hard work, it also taught him that women were demanding and perfectionistic. *Playboy's* values stated that "perfect" women want men who have Porsches, Rolexes, and Armani suits.

Neither system promoted the inner value of the person as a human being. Robert had to learn this on his own. He had to discover that people could be valued in their own right and that he could be valued for just being Robert, warts and all.

Someone Right for You

The idea that marriages are made in heaven and romance happens by magic is only a myth. Sure, some people fall in love by bumping into each other on a crowded subway, marry within two weeks, and live happily ever after. And some people do indeed win the lottery. Are you willing to wait to win the lottery for your next meal? Are you willing to wait for magic, a fairy godmother, or a bolt of lightening to find your partner in life?

The approach in this book to finding someone right for you combined personal understanding and growth with action. Insight and introspection alone are not enough; action is required to overcome old, ineffective ways of thinking and behaving. Following the strategies I have described, you can develop a plan for finding a perfect partner. And don't, for a minute, think there is only one possible partner out there who is right for you—there are many.

There are three levels of involvement with the strategies presented in this book. Each will enhance your self-esteem and increase your chances of success.

(1)   Reading the book will change your way of thinking.

(2)   Doing the exercises will increase your self-understanding.

(3)   Following the strategies will alter your life.

You learned a great deal about yourself and relationships by reading this book, even if you stop there. Your thinking was challenged; your beliefs questioned; discrepancies between your words and your behavior confronted. Having read this book, you can begin to leave codependent relationships and loneliness behind. You no longer have to be powerless to find satisfying interpersonal relationships. You can take charge of your romantic life and make things happen while maintaining your own personal style.

You will benefit even more when you have completed the exercises and decide to put what you have learned into practice. Doing the exercises will give you a clearer understanding of your strengths and weaknesses. You will learn how others see you. Then you can compare their perceptions with yours.

Everyone wants intimacy. But the closeness we seek is elusive. Once we find it, we have difficulty maintaining it. Often we fear it, too. Intimacy with others begins with self-intimacy; you can only be as intimate with others as you are with yourself. As you do the exercises, rember that you are not alone. Even the most intimidating person wants intimacy.

You are on a journey of self-discovery. Discover your blind-spots. Like the six people you met in this book, learn more about what it is you are searching for and how to achieve it. Just as Darwin, who once said, "if I see more than others, it is because I stand on the shoulders of giants," you will learn from others.

They said it couldn't be done; you now know differently. You have learned the secret for integrating romance and love with the practical considerations of a relationship. It is possible and you can make romance happen.